ONE SILENT VOICE

THE JEANNIE SINGLETON STORY

NICOLE & ROBERT DU SHANE

HOPKIN'S HOUSE
PUBLISHING

One Silent Voice: The Jeannie Singleton Story

Copyright © 2015 - 2018 by Nicole & Robert Du Shane

For author contact information visit :

http://www.OneSilentVoice.com

Book and Cover design by Robert Du Shane

ISBN: 978-1-945175-97-8

Library of Congress CIP data applied for.

First Edition: December 2015

CONTENTS

INTRODUCTION:

HOW THIS BOOK CAME TO BE.

I would like to start out by saying that One Silent Voice: Jeannie Singleton Story will always remain high on my list as the most interesting and heartbreaking stories of my writing career. I would never have guessed by the completion of this book I would be consumed by a little girl that I never met, or that I would make new friends that I will never forget.

I was first made aware of Jeannie Singleton when my husband Robert and I were in the Kalamazoo Public Library scouring the local history section for possible stories to include in an upcoming Kalamazoo book. Rob was searching for the word "mystery" in the library's electronic newspaper index and buried within the list of other local and state oddities, a 1985 article title captured our attention: 30 Years; Still Unsolved.

My husband and I are both lovers of history and true crime. It was no wonder that this case would grab our attention. We were however surprised to discover just how much this story had taken hold. Following the discovery of that article; Jeannie became the primary focus for the remainder of our time in Kalamazoo.

We spent the remainder of the afternoon scouring the newspaper archives and saving as many Kalamazoo Gazette newspaper articles as we could find. Following our visit to the library, Rob and I not only took a drive to Blakeslee Street where Jeannie lived (her house was torn down decades ago), but we also started out on a quest to find her final resting place based on 1955 news articles. We did manage to find her grave, which was not an easy task in a snow-covered cemetery, especially when you take into account the fact that Mt. Ever-Rest Cemetery changed the two large bible statues mentioned in 1955 due to storm damage; and that these statues were our only waypoints by which to start our search.

The discovery of her grave had a spiritual twist for me. We had been searching for nearly an hour on a cold winters' day. Rob and I were about ready to give up and come back in the spring. Out of frustration, I said out loud, "Jeannie, I am trying to find you. Can you please help me out?"

I literally took 10 more steps, looked down and there it was, the grave of this newly beloved girl. We quickly removed the remaining snow covering her grave marker and put an artificial red flower near the top; the flower we placed had been blown against my leg just seconds after asking Jeannie for help.

We stood there, looking down on the final resting place of this little angel and were filled with immense sadness. Later that night we both returned home, but Jeannie never left us.

The next day I posted a small message about Jeannie on the Vanished Kalamazoo Facebook page. I was soon thrilled to see a comment posted by Robert Holderbaum, who claimed to have been the last child to see Jeannie alive that day. My heart raced with possibilities and an internet-based friendship soon developed between Bob and me. I talked to Bob, and he naturally supported my ideas of writing Jeannie's story, He eventually became an intricate part in the book's creation.

Throughout the following months, Jeannie was never far from my mind. I would work on other books, but her story and face continued to haunt me. I felt a powerful connection with this unfortunate little girl. Jeannie and I may have been born twenty-three years apart. However, she and I were fated similarly. Few know why but in many ways I am that little girl. In some ways I lived Jeannie's tragedy; I was just lucky enough to be able to live to tell of it. I have special prayers for Jeannie. I know Heaven gained a beautiful angel that day in 1955.

As time passed my obsession grew and I became more determined to obtain the police files related to Jeannie's case. I was not overly optimistic about how many of the records would be preserved after close to six decades had passed. I, however, was of the mindset that anything was better than nothing.

Bob and I discussed our next move, and it was decided by both of us, but initiated by Bob. We would file a petition under the Freedom of

Information Act for copies of Jeannie's case files. We silently kept our fingers crossed.

Thirty days later, we received our answer - the petition was denied. I accepted this initial roadblock in stride, despite knowing I would never have enough to carry an entire book to completion with only newspaper articles and my witty personality.

I expressed my disappointment to Bob and my now-husband Rob, but I was determined to petition again at a later date. Like Tim Robbin's character in the Shawshank Redemption movie, we were prepared to send in repeated requests; they couldn't ignore us forever!

The next day we received a second denial letter. Seriously, one wasn't good enough!?

Unexpectedly, this letter would soon make my disappointment turn into amazed speculation. It was a denial letter. However, the official reason for denial was the case of Jeannie Singleton became reopened due to renewed interest!

You can just imagine the elation after learning a cold case team was investigating this 60-year-old crime. We were all ecstatic with possibilities but also frustrated as Bob, and I knew this project would probably have to be placed on hold.

It would be a small book if it were only based off of newspaper articles, a few former classmates of Jeannie's, and my writing skills. Forty-five days later another request for case files was sent out; we didn't hold out much hope this time.

In all honesty, I think I quit breathing for a few moments when first Rob called, and then Bob emailed me and informed me the petition was approved. We were only given a 30-day window to pay for the files! We were duly advised in the letter that if the 30 days lapsed, we would not be given this opportunity again.

Of course, I jumped on this with great excitement and three days after the approved letter was received, the files were paid for and obtained. Honestly, I forfeited paying my electric bill that month, so I could get my hands on this file! With this thick case file now sitting in my hot little hands, I was so consumed that I went through every piece of paper within hours; as did Rob. That was not an easy task as we were granted over a 300-page file! I have a sneaking suspicion that Bob also did the same with his copy.

Reading case reports of Jeannie's autopsy was gut-wrenching to say the very least. Many times I would have to put down the reports and cry. For two people who love true crime books and television, Rob and I both found it hard to read the forensic reality that was sitting in front of our face. When you watch these cases on TV, it's a very aesthetic view of the facts, but this was different. There was nothing that could dull the anguish and horror young Jeannie felt during her last moments on Earth; there was nothing that could buffer Rob and me from imagining this horror based on the written word presented to us.

Throughout the next couple of years Rob and I have talked with numerous former classmates, members of Jeannie's family, members of the Prolo family, surviving 1955 police officers and current detectives. At times I would think about Bob Holderbaum and wonder how it affects him to read the case file. Does it make his thoughts rush back to 1955 and that horrible day? I can only visualize May and June of 1955 as a third-person; Bob, however, lived through all of this.

Our hearts will forever go out to the family of Jeannie Singleton, and all parents and siblings that have lost a child through similar circumstances. We know there are more cases such as Jeannie's; some still remain unsolved right here in Michigan. Our prayers will forever be with those victims and with their families who had to discover a new way to live on.

-Nicole Du Shane

MEET GLORIA JEAN SINGLETON

Gloria Jean "Jeannie" Singleton was born on November 1, 1946. This beautiful baby girl was welcomed by her siblings with love and excitement; life was good in the Singleton household; until at the young age of four, Jeannie was faced with a possibly fatal disease.

Jeannie became ill from what was often reported as Rheumatic fever. Rheumatic fever is an autoimmune disease, often contracted after a strep infection that in many cases results in death.

With all of the complications of Rheumatic Fever (which we will discuss in the next chapter), it was a small miracle that Jeannie survived the disease as well as she did.

Despite the physical impairments brought on by her illness, not the least of which, the fact that she had one leg shorter than the other, she was far from the "cripple" the media often described her as after her disappearance.

Jeannie was energetic and strived to never allow anything to stop her from playing like any other healthy child would. Her one set back? Sometimes she would have to take a break to rest. This was little wonder since she suffered from an enlarged heart; a condition that would tire her young body more quickly than her peers.

When we interviewed childhood friends, Judi Nufer and Brenda Lyles, they both commented on how Jeannie was fearless when it came to physical activities like roller skating and biking. Judi summed it up best when she said: "Jeannie and I would skate until our feet hurt!"

Brenda added to this sediment when she recalled a time when she and Jeannie only had one set of roller skates. Not to be discouraged, each girl took one skate. The little daredevils then skated down Blakeslee hill.

Brenda jokingly stated while recalling the event: "You can imagine it didn't end well!"

In a neighborhood that primarily consisted of boys, Jeannie spent as much time as possible with her female cohorts.

Jeannie did have one life-long infliction that seems to have been a psychological effect of her rheumatic fever. She would pick at any bump or sore on her body, and then cry out for ointments to soothe her. Skin rashes, lesions, and bumps are a common symptom of the disease, and subconsciously Jeannie probably recalls how everyone gave her ointments to relieve the pain and discomfort. At that early age, her mind made a vital connection and related ointment to a soothing, comforting feeling. She would purposely cause a reaction that would require the desired comfort of ointment and attention for the rest of her short life.

While the world loves a bubbly happy child, there is a serious drawback to that personality in some children; naivety. Jeannie had been scolded several times for talking to strange adults while walking home from school or out playing with her friends. She was prone to walking around the neighborhood and talking to all the grownups who would listen to her. Despite warnings from parents, siblings and numerous friends, Jeannie never truly believed in her heart that anyone would hurt her. Young Jeannie was very compassionate and loved the world and all the people in it. Unluckily for Jeannie that was an ill-fated flaw that would soon be used to someone's sick advantage.

Jeannie did have one very obvious physical condition as a result of her illness. She had one leg that was noticeably shorter than the other. Her parents Dorothy and Steve Singleton were working very hard to save the money needed to correct this issue for Jeannie. We now wonder, with a heavy heart, if the hard-earned funds intended to help their beloved daughter return to normalcy, ended up going instead to her funeral.

Nevertheless, Jeannie made a lasting impression on all who knew her. It's unfortunate that those lasting memories are now mixed with feelings of tragedy and injustice. Lest we never forget: Jeannie Singleton was a happy, vibrant 8-year-old girl, not just another crime statistic. Her happiness continues to live on through surviving siblings, friends, former classmates and teachers and thanks to this book; she will now live in the minds of all of you.

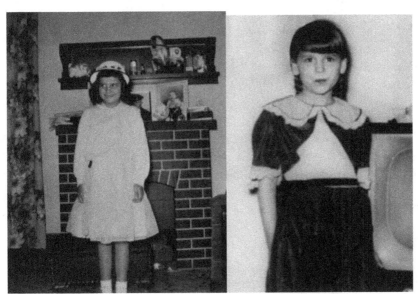

Undated photos of Gloria Jean "Jeannie" Singleton.
From the authors' private collection.

RHEUMATIC FEVER OR POLIO?

Most of the police reports report that Jeannie had suffered from Rheumatic fever, a disease that presents most often as inflammatory lesions that develop in the connective tissues. The inflammation is most often present in the connective tissues of the heart and joints.

Rheumatic fever is a rarity today in the United States. This is due to advances in the medical field that led to the development of proactive measures to prevent the fever from occurring following a strep infection. The disease is still not beaten, however. Death tolls continue to be high in children living in underdeveloped countries, due to the lack of proper healthcare and antibiotics.

The first signs of rheumatic fever are painful and swollen joints; so poor Jeannie was inflicted with even more pain and discomfort after dealing with her strep throat. Many medical websites explain the joints can become so painful that something as light as a bed sheet or clothing can become excruciating.

To combat this illness, Jeannie would have been given strong antibiotics as well as cardiac medications. The latter given as a result of the swelling of the heart that was a critical condition caused by the fever. Despite these medications, Jeannie, unfortunately, suffered lifelong cardiac issues, according to her brother Steve who we interviewed via phone.

We were further informed that she suffered from an enlarged heart at the time of her passing. This is a typical condition among long-term sufferers of damaged heart valves. Regrettably, if she had never been abducted, Jeannie still may very well have suffered a shortened lifespan marred by cardiac issues and possible strokes.

It is stated several times in the police reports that Jeannie suffered stunted growth in one leg due to rheumatic fever. This condition puzzled us. We decided to look further into the symptoms of Rheumatic fever. It was during this research that we came across a puzzling piece of information on the Mayo Clinic's website, where it was stated; "Rheumatic fever does not cause long-term bone and joint damage."

We decided to contact Dr. Eileen Crimmins, Professor of Gerontology at the University of Southern California. Dr. Crimmins was awarded the Kleemeier Award for her research in childhood infections & diseases that affects us as we age. When we asked about shortened legs caused by rheumatic fever in a 4-year-old, her exact reply to our question was:

> "I am sorry, but I have not heard of shorter legs as an outcome of rheumatic fever; we have seen heart consequences. This sounds like polio."

While reading further into the Jeannie Singleton case files, we found references that she had suffered from polio, not from rheumatic fever. We knew immediately this disease was more crippling than rheumatic fever, not that rheumatic fever wasn't bad enough. Could Jeannie have suffered from polio instead of rheumatic fever?

This is a question somewhat explained by a recent event in our own lives. We recently found out that Nicole's maternal grandmother had polio at the age of 3. This is the same grandma that Nicole had often asked about as a child.

"Why does Grandma walk funny?'

Polio reared its ugly head in the US in the summer of 1916. The epidemic swept through 26 states; New York is the hardest hit. By July 1, 1916, 350 children in New York City alone had been paralyzed by the disease and 75 more children had died. By the end of the sixth day of July, despite the cancellations of all Independence Day celebrations from July 2-4th, New York City was faced by 240 more inflicted children. Since polio was most dangerous during the summer months, the cool air of October 1916 was a blessing. Unfortunately, that blessing came too late for the 27,000 victims who contracted polio and the 6,000 who had already perished within a few short months.

Polio soon became the world's most feared disease. It would hit without warning and required long quarantine periods where parents were separated from their children. The majority of victims were children between the ages of 5 - 9 years old. Those who survived were plagued by a life filled with wheelchairs, leg braces, crutches, breathing devices and deformed limbs.

Polio would not only cause paralysis or arms, legs, and half the body but for thousands it would paralyze the lungs, destroying the body's ability to breathe. On October 12, 1928, the Children's Hospital in Boston created the first Iron Lung machine. Iron lungs worked by continually raising and lowering the pressure in the apparatus, which expanded and contracted the lungs, mimicking normal breathing.

Thousands of lives were saved by this device, but only the lucky few. Iron lungs were very expensive. The cost of these machines was $1,500 – the price of an average home in 1930. The cost of running the device on a daily basis was also a huge factor. The families of some patients would spend many years or in some cases the rest of their lives paying for this expensive treatment. This was an expense many families couldn't take on, especially since even with an iron lung, the fatality rate still exceeded 80%.

Another common side effect of Polio was an enlarged heart. This condition was caused by issues in the lungs. When the body has to use more effort to breathe the heart also becomes overworked and begins to enlarge.

Understandably, panic grew throughout the nation. This was especially true during the summer months when the disease is the strongest. The public didn't understand the illness, and this led to many wacky theories about how the Polio was spread. During this time the Department of Health was bombarded with questions about seemingly unbelievable methods they believed this plague was being spread.

Some of the many theories that were widely accepted were:
- High groundwater
- Ice-cream cones
- Excavations
- Flies
- Mosquitoes (at least this one was halfway logical!)
- Bedbugs

- Rats
- Filthy sewers
- Street dust
- Cornflakes
- The subway
- Parasites in the water
- Alloys in cooking utensils
- Gases from munitions factories
- The bent-over position children assumed at school desks
- White clothing
- Earthquakes
- Volcanoes
- Mercury poisoning
- Electrical disturbances
- Sunburns
- Intestinal or bowel obstructions
- Secondhand bedding
- Rotten Food
- Excessive glare
- Dirty milk bottles
- Carrying coins in the mouth
- Tobacco
- Cats (this theory led to the destruction of more than 70,000 cats in New York in one month!)

The polio outbreak wasn't limited to one social class. In fact future President Franklin D. Roosevelt contracted polio a few years before he was elected to office; a diagnosis that nearly ended his political career. FDR would instead draw strength from his personal victory over Polio and would go on to not only be our first "handicap" president but also the longest serving US president.

The summer of 1952 saw the worst outbreak of Polio in the nation's history. Nearly 58,000 Americans, mostly children, contracted the disease. Thousands of children lives were cut tragically short and never lived to see another summer.

On April 15th, 1955, media and medical professionals alike all crowded into Rackham Lecture Hall at the University of Michigan for a huge announcement. Jonas Salk, who had spent the early 1940s working as a professor's assistant at the University of Michigan, announced to the world a true miracle he had developed a polio vaccine.

This new vaccine proved to be 80% effective to those who currently had polio and prevented the contraction of the diseased from the people not afflicted. Reporters and physicians interviewed for the 1955 newspapers commented that they could feel a weight being suddenly lifted off the country's shoulders.

Considering the facts that Jeannie's right leg was shorter than her left leg, that she needed to use leg braces, and that her brother reported to us that she had an enlarged heart. We feel it is very likely that polio was probably the real culprit that led to her disability.

ONE FATEFUL DAY

A hot, muggy Monday morning greeted the Singleton family at 1310 Blakeslee in Kalamazoo, Michigan on May 23rd, 1955. On this unseasonably warm day, 8-year-old Gloria Jean, known to everyone as "Jeannie," chose to wear a pink plaid dress and a new pair of multi-colored sandals. Mary Singleton, the eldest Singleton child, brushed Jeannie's hair and pulled it back into a ponytail. Jeannie asked if she could wear one of her mother's kerchiefs in her hair but was told no. However, since Mary was in the 8th grade, Jeannie had to leave for school almost 15 minutes ahead of the younger siblings. Jeannie apparently took this opportunity to disobey her eldest sister as she snuck the kerchief out of the house anyway.

The morning progressed like any other. The Singleton children left for school, Dorothy, the Singleton mother, was driven by her husband Steve that up to the street on Blakeslee to the Kalamazoo Tuberculosis Hospital's Northwest Unit where she was continuing her nursing education. Since Steve didn't have to work until later in the day, he remained home with their youngest child.

Jeannie happily traveled down the streets to the Woodward Elementary School building; accompanying her was her best friend, 8-year-old Mary Heinie and Jeannie's brother Steve.

Despite the unusually high temperature for May, everyone was in good spirits. Jeannie was having a great day, animatedly showing off her new footwear to all her friends and teachers. When lunchtime approached, she walked back home with Mary as she usually did. On this day however one girl apparently ate lunch faster than the other as Mary and Jeannie traveled back to school separately.

Businesses ran, as usual, household chores were being accomplished, and plans of planting gardens and going fishing were on everyone's minds on this warm afternoon. Not one thought was centered on violence or predators that may be lurking their streets. The unassuming innocence of Kalamazoo life in 1955 was about to be shattered, and children were about to learn that real monsters do exist.

Around 3:30pm, school bells throughout the city rang in unison and children excitedly exited their schools and ran for their buses or homes, eager to play outside with their friends.

Steve Singleton loaded their 4-year-old son, Chuck, into the car and drove up the hill to the hospital to pick up his wife. Dorothy finished with her clinical studies for the day, hopped into their vehicle and all three family members traveled downtown to go grocery shopping.

Little Steve noticed Jeannie standing outside of the school building and asked if she wanted to walk home with him. She declined, stating she wanted to wait for her friend. Assuming Jeannie was talking about her best friend Mary he left Jeannie at school and raced towards home.

During an interview with Steve in 2013, he sadly stated that he never really forgave himself for leaving Jeannie at school that day. Forty-nine years did nothing to relieve the feelings of guilt. Whoever this friend was, it later became clear it was not Mary, stood Jeannie up and she was forced to begin her walk home by herself.

Eleanor King, 1034 W. North Street, reports to police that she saw Jeannie, "or a person closely resembling her description," talking to a man in front of Jacquay's Market on North Street. The police report indicated that King said Jeannie "seemed to be absorbed in the man's conversation, was laughing and joking with him." King also provided police with a description of a 55 - 60-year old man, and characterized him as "a typical grandfather type." It was never proven if Ms. King did indeed see Jeannie or if this was another young girl walking the neighborhood.

It would have been after this alleged sighting that Singleton family friend Reda Raynes, on her way to a doctor's office visit, came upon Jeannie standing at the drinking fountain on the southeast corner of Douglas and North streets, she noticed the young girl was walking alone. Stopping for a few minutes to chat, Jeannie excitedly showed her grown-up friend her new sandals while waiting for the crossing guard to help her across the busy streets.

Crossing guard, August Cook, later stated to police that he assisted Jeannie across North Street, and then across west towards the opposite side of Douglas. He noted that Jeannie was alone at this time, but there were a few kids that crossed before her and were walking up Douglas Street as well.

Fourth-grader Robert "Bob" Holderbaum was one of the children walking ahead of Jeannie on that day. Jeannie was approximately 200 feet behind him. Young Jeannie called out to the neighborhood boy and walked as fast as she could to meet up with him. Jeannie again had a new person to show off her latest pride and joy – her multi-colored sandals. Bob Holderbaum, now a Battle Creek resident, says he can still vividly remember those sandals; a memory that has always haunted him throughout his life.

The two Woodward school children chatted while they walked the short distance north on Douglas Street until they came to the corner of Blakeslee and Douglas. With Bob living six houses further ahead on Douglas, he extended his goodbye to Jeannie, even perhaps telling her he would see her at school. Jeannie's house was located roughly 300 feet heading west up Blakeslee hill, and Bob noted that he saw her start up the hill heading towards home. I have often wondered if Bob, to this day, is filled with "what-ifs." What if he had merely looked back – would he have seen something?

Chances are nothing would have been changed by a simple glance back. Unfortunately at some point within those 300 feet up Blakeslee hill, on a hot late spring afternoon, second-grader Jeannie Singleton encountered a monster and would never be seen alive again.

Undated photo of the Singleton home
Photo courtesy of MLive Media Group & the Kalamazoo Gazette

THE BEGINNING OF A
NIGHTMARE

Jeannie's sisters Mary and Patsy were at the Blakeslee residence before 4:00pm as they were almost every day in preparation for the remaining children to return from school. Mary had begun her usual chores and was washing the breakfast dishes when Jimmy came home and then dashed back out again to play with the neighborhood boys. She vaguely noticed that Jeannie was not with him but thought nothing more of it as Jeannie would sometimes go to a friend's house before returning home. In fact, two years prior, Jeannie gave her parents quite the scare when she had not returned home from school. In this case, she was discovered over two hours later at a friend's house a block away.

When Mary Heinie visited the Singleton residence around 4:20pm to give Jeannie back the books she had left the week before at the Heinie residence, having Jeannie not home yet was not a concern. Jeannie had several friends around the neighborhood, not just little Mary. Everyone automatically assumed Jeannie had ventured off once again to play with a friend. "Jeannie will come home soon," big sister Mary told herself. "She always does."

The remaining Singleton children came home and immediately went outdoors to play; Patsy staying behind to help Mary prepare dinner. With the food complete, Mary called all the kids in for supper but noticed immediately that Jeannie was still not among them. Jeannie's brother Steve offered to run down to Mary Heinie's house to see if Jeannie was there. She wasn't.

After the parents completed their shopping, Steve and "Chucky" dropped Dorothy off to her place of employment at Grace's Nursing Home on South Park Street, and then returned home. Steve worked delivery at the Kalamazoo Vegetable Parchment Company during the daytime. The family was used to Dorothy having to work second shift at the nursing home, so the eldest children learned to pitch in to help take care of their younger siblings. Steve Singleton returned home with

Chucky, and he fell asleep on the couch without joining the family for dinner. He never noticed Jeannie's plate still waiting for her in front of an empty chair.

After the dinner dishes were washed, Mary began her task of completing math homework but found it hard to concentrate as Jeannie still had not appeared. Now she was starting to get worried and sent the eldest brother Jimmy to see if Jeannie was at a neighborhood friend's house.

It was close to 8:00pm when Jimmy returned and informed his older sister that he could not find Jeannie anywhere; none of her friends saw her after school. Mary entered the living room and attempted to wake up her father. Steve was so tired that none of his daughter's words made any sense and he proceeded to fall back asleep.

When 8:30pm came, Mary knew this could not wait any longer and insistently woke her father up and explained that Jeannie never came home from school. This time his daughter's words registered in his foggy mind, and he jumped up from the couch and left the house ten minutes later to inform Dorothy of the situation.

Dorothy did what any mother would do-she immediately left work and insisted that she and Steve drive through the neighborhoods, hoping they would spot Jeannie playing in a neighbor's yard.

In another part of the city around the time the parents returned home without seeing their daughter, Officer Middaugh of the Kalamazoo Police Department was on his routine patrol. Knowing that humid and warm nights typically brings with it higher rates of criminal activity, he watched the sun disappear over the horizon and prayed for a quiet evening. At approximately 9:30pm, he received a call from dispatch about a missing child report coming from the 1310 Blakeslee Street address. He knew right then his night was about to become busier, but he had no premonition of the case he was about to be involved in.

Upon arrival at the Singleton residence, the first person he spoke with was Dorothy, who informed him her daughter Jeannie had not returned home from school, and her whereabouts unknown. The officer wrote down a description of the young girl then returned to his vehicle to radio dispatch. A description of Jeannie and what she was wearing earlier in the day was broadcast to every police officer in the city of Kalamazoo.

With the information given by Dorothy, another officer at the Kalamazoo Police station called Jeannie's teacher for more information. The distraught educator informed police that Jeannie had in fact attended school that day and left after school was over. Nothing out of the ordinary occurred or was noticed; Jeannie was her usual bubbly self that day.

Armed with this new information, Officer Middaugh asked one of the Singleton brothers to accompany him in his patrol car and point out where Jeannie's neighborhood friends live. The case file never specified which brother joined the police officer that night, but regardless of that missing fact, Jeannie was not present at any of the houses. Middaugh dropped the sibling back off at home and assured the parents that every officer will be looking for her, but please inform them when Jeannie returned home later or arrived at school the next day.

Officer Middaugh's shift ended at 11:00pm, but he decided to join Officer Growden who was just beginning his shift to help in the search. This compassionate officer began to have a bad feeling about this missing child's case and wanted to continue, off the clock, looking for Jeannie. Together the two officers retraced the route Jeannie walked home from Woodward School, checked the stores at the corner of Douglas and North Street, and continued checking all the surrounding streets. Around 3:30am, Officer Middaugh, growing tired, decided to call it a night and was taken back to his personal car at the police station. As he drove home, he silently prayed that Jeannie Singleton would be discovered safe the next day; just another example of how children can unintentionally stress out their parents.

The Singleton family was praying for that too.

Robert Holdenbaum showing a police officer where he
last recalls seeing Jeannie.
Photo courtesy of MLive Media Group, & the Kalamazoo Gazette.

Steve Singleton discussing the case with Kalamazoo Police.
Photo courtesy of MLive Media Group, & the Kalamazoo Gazette.

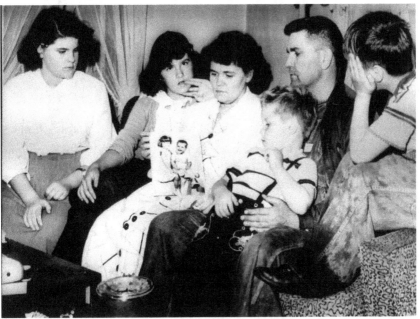

Mrs. Singleton holds up a photo of their missing
daughter Jeannie, while the family looks on.
From the authors' private collection

"OPERATION JEANNIE"

May 24, 1955

Police Captain Riley Stewart arrived at work early in the morning hoping for some good news. When he was informed that Jeannie Singleton had not appeared at school that morning, he knew in his gut this case may not end well. He rounded up all his officers and detectives in a meeting room and prepared them for the next step – searches and questioning everyone in and around the Blakeslee neighborhood.

Time was of the essence. The majority of stranger abductions of children cases last 24 hours or less, after this time there is a 60% chance the child will be found murdered. Jeannie had now been missing for approximately 16 hours. These statistics ran through the minds of every police officer in the room that morning. All they knew is Jeannie had to be found soon if she was to be saved.

News of the missing girl spread very quickly throughout Kalamazoo County and tore at the heartstrings of many. By 1:00pm, newspapers throughout Michigan ran a story about Jeannie's disappearance. Hundreds of local citizens began contacting the Kalamazoo Police Department offering their assistance in the search. The search was given a name by authorities - "Operation Jeannie," which officially commenced after the Kalamazoo City Police Department and Detectives Bureau ended their morning briefing.

One credible tip did come during the early morning hour of 4:00 am. Leona Webster was on Ruth Street when she noticed a 1950-1952 Chevy parked in front of a house. The driver of the car was standing outside of the vehicle, and with the interior dome light on. She could tell there was a young girl, approximately 7 or 8 years old wearing a pink dress, sitting in the front seat.

Leona described the young man as having bushy light brown or red hair, wearing a dark-colored jacket and light colored pants. When the man noticed Leona, he reached inside the car and turned off the lights. The man continued to stand there and watch her until she felt uncomfortable and left. Unfortunately, she was never able to obtain any numbers on the vehicle plates.

This lead was discussed and assigned to a couple of officers and the morning meeting continued.

It was decided by Captain Stewart that numerous officers would be pulled from their regular duties and reassigned to search party responsibilities. Some principal officers would be in charge of the search areas for community volunteers, while other officers were ordered to perform house-to-house searches for Jeannie or any evidence that Jeannie may have been there. Officers from other areas of Kalamazoo County were utilized to help cover the City of Kalamazoo since the police force suddenly found themselves extraordinarily understaffed and need help to provide protection for the rest of the citizens.

In mid-morning hours, concerned community members who volunteered for search parties were briefed by Officers Smith, Kincaid, Thorsen, Priest and Sergeant Ragan on proper search techniques, and informed of the areas they were to be assigned to search. They were further instructed to notify the officer on the scene of anything suspicious and to assist the officer in bagging any item that may be considered relevant.

Detective Burl McCarty was assigned the duty of visiting the Singleton household to interview the parents once again. He noticed several additional cars parked on Blakeslee Street and correctly guessed they were friends of the victim's family. Det. McCarty was escorted into the house and introduced to Mr. and Mrs. J.D. Lyles, who were good friends of the Singleton family; their daughter Brenda was a close friend of

Jeannie's. The other person present in the living room was Leslie Hume Jr.

The parents turned over to the detective a dress belonging to Jeannie. It was a mate to the dress she was wearing the previous day to school. Det. McCarty wrote down a more detailed description of the pink and plaid dress. It was at this time while touching her missing daughter's clothes that Dorothy broke into tears and explained that she and Steve both constantly warned Jeannie about talking to or getting into cars with strangers. In her next breath, Dorothy's voice broke when she confessed to spoiling Jeannie more than the other children because her daughter suffered from the effects of her illness. Steve just looked away, determined to keep up a strong image for his anguished wife.

Detective McCarty decided to change the subject and resumed his questioning about friends or other people Jeannie may visit in the neighborhood. Dorothy remembered that her girls and other neighborhood girls had been going down to Summit Street and visiting with an old man named James Walker.

With the duplicate of Jeannie's dress in hand, the detective returned to his car and radioed for the nearest officer to accompany him to the Walker residence on Summit. When he arrived on Summit, he was joined by Detectives Yankee and Aldrich and Officer Earl Ex.

James Walker, age 86, opened his door to the detectives and welcomed them into his home. He explained that he lived alone the majority of the time due to one son working as a well driller and was often gone on assignments, and his other son had been an inmate of the Kalamazoo State Hospital for the last 24 years.

Detective Yankee decided to turn this questioning to a more personal level. James answered these questions very openly and explained he had been married twice, the first time for a little over 23 years until her death. He then married his boyhood sweetheart and remained with her for an additional 23 years, until her death six years ago. He admitted that he continued to have intercourse with his second wife until her death and despite both of his late wives' illnesses; he had always remained faithful to both.

Mr. Walker did become slightly agitated when asked directly about the neighborhood girls visits to him. He angrily denied ever messing around with the young girls that come to his house. Some neighborhood kids who had previously spoken to Detectives Aldrich and Yankee while circulating throughout the neighborhood had commented that James Walker would have the girls sit on his lap and he would constantly give the girls kisses. When asked about these comments being made by girls to the police, Mr. Walker became angrier and stated that he just loved children and he didn't think he was doing anything wrong.

James Walker agreed to allow the four men to search his house. No evidence pertaining to Jeannie was located anywhere in the house, so they apologized for the intrusion and left the old man's residence.

Detective Yankee and Officer Ex continued to take statements from neighborhood residents. The first statement of the day came from Mrs. Griffin from 1213 Blakeslee who stated the old man who lives in the house behind hers, at 815 Douglas Avenue, was Arthur Schilling. Schilling, according to Ms. Griffin, has been known to molest little girls. "Not only that, but Jeannie knew this man, and I have seen her be friendly with him," continued Mrs. Griffin. After this bold piece of information, the woman did admit that she had not seen Jeannie or Arthur Schilling that particular afternoon.

Two houses down at 1217 Blakeslee, Mrs. Shorter, did inform the detective she had seen Mr. Schilling yesterday. He had been working in his yard all afternoon. Thanking Mrs. Shorter for her cooperation, Detective Yankee took down the information. A background search on Arthur Schilling came back with the information that Mr. Schilling was indeed a convicted sex offender, he immediately became a likely suspect for Jeannie's disappearance. After questioning of Mr. Schilling, plus a thorough search of his home, the police wrote him off as the main suspect.

Mrs. Jennie Masaillia, at 1301 Blakeslee, informed the detective that she witnessed Jennie riding her bike across the street from her house around 4:00pm yesterday afternoon. The woman stated she was positive she saw the girl. When the police questioned the rest of the residents on Blakeslee, it was discovered that no one except for Mrs. Masaillia witnessed this alleged event.

Another likely suspect soon came to the attention of the investigators. This suspect was 14-year-old John Creek. John lived nearby at 1318 Blakeslee. Even at this young age, John had already been arrested for sex offenses. The offense he had been arrested for was possession of pornographic material and pleasuring himself in public.

When the detective met up with John, the teenager stated he left St. Augustine School and walked over to Woodward school to meet up with his girlfriend, Joyce. He walked Joyce home on Cobb Street, leaving her residence at 4:00pm and arriving home shortly afterward. John Creek's father confirmed leaving the house at 4:10pm and passing his son as he began driving down their street. Neither John Creek nor his father remembers seeing Jeannie walking on Blakeslee yesterday afternoon. The teenager was written off as a possible suspect as it was deemed improbable he could have abducted Jeannie within a 10-minute window of time.

Detective Yankee was then instructed to follow up on a complaint on Clarence Street. Mrs. Richards informed authorities she spotted a green car driving around the corner of Clarence and Vine. Inside of the car she had noted a screaming girl who was attempting to get out of the car. The driver pulled the girl back into her seat and continued to drive down Vine Street. Soon she spotted the car pull into a parking lot at the end of Vine Street and watched the girl begin to scream and try to flee the car again. Mrs. Richards was able to give the detective the license plate number of the car.

Following this tip, Det. Yankee called in the license number and located the owner; Robert Staley. Robert resided at 1101 James Street. Det. Yankee's hopes that this may be a good lead were soon dashed when he learned that Robert and his wife Dee had been in the area mentioned in the complaint and were having a heated argument. Dee confirmed she had been trying to leave the car. When she was finally able to exit the car, she walked to her mother's house. Mrs. Staley readily admitted that she had been the one screaming as well.

While detectives were chasing leads and questioning neighbors, nearly 150 Western Michigan University students took the opportunity offered to them by their school to aid in the search for little Jeannie. Led by Sergeant C. Adams and accompanied by twelve other officers, this ambitious group spent their day battling muggy and sometimes rainy 80-degree weather to search over a nine square mile area north of Ravine Road, west to Nichols Rd, and as far east as Douglas Ave. Other students aided the police department by searching the gravel pits located behind the A.M. Todd Company on Douglas Avenue, with the assistance of four police officers.

No matter how exhausted or wet these Western students became they chose to not give up. Pressing on, these determined young people moved to West Michigan Avenue and covered everything from the railroad tracks on Old West Michigan Ave, beyond the golf course, and then south to Winchell Ave.

Sergeant Ragan led a group of community volunteers to search Red Arrow Park and the surrounding areas, which included Factory Street and Miller Road which included Pattimiller Woods [sic], which is possibly modern-day Hayes Park, plus an area east of Olmstead Road which is along the Davis River.

A group of 25 Boy Scouts, led by their den leaders and Officer Kincaid, searched Angel Field and the pistol range which were located on Red Arrow Highway.

Officer Smith led a group of searchers to cover the rear of Borgess Hospital and the dump behind the Sutherland Mill.

Officer Priest took charge of a team of volunteers to cover a huge area of Kings Highway which included a dump area behind Security Home Supply and later a dump site on Ravine Road. While this was being accomplished, Officer Morrison searched another dump site on the south side of Kings Highway. The group also searched the area leading up to the railroad tracks, and the vicinity of the Panelite Company, including the numerous disposal ponds located east of Burdick Street.

Amidst of all the ground searches, the Civil Air Patrol deployed 5 planes that circled overhead hoping to spot some trace of Jeannie in fields, parks or along riverbanks. An anonymous tip was called in that someone witnessed a man dumping a large bundle in the Consumers Sand & Gravel Company's quarries which were located near the corner of Nazareth Road & East Main Street. The lead sent searchers into the area in force. Armed with large searchlights loaned by the Naval Reserves, searchers waded through the waist-deep slimy water while others combed the entire excavation site in hopes of locating some clue. Not one shred of evidence, or sign of this mysterious bundle, surfaced during the three-hour search.

By 1:00 am everyone was wet, filthy, sweaty and hungry, but determined to try again tomorrow. No one wanted to give up that day, but deep down they knew continuous searches in darkness would be futile.

The physical and mental condition of the missing girl pushed predominately forward in their thoughts when a steady rain began, and the air temperature plummeted. Everyone was haunted by visions of a girl wandering around outside feeling scared, hungry and increasingly cold as she became soaked in the rain. With heavy hearts, they returned to their own warm homes.

In a lit-up house on Blakeslee Street, Steve and Dorothy hugged their children goodnight and prepared to endure the second night without their daughter, trying hard not be haunted by those same thoughts.

May 25, 1955

Within the next 24 hours, everyone in Michigan knew about a young girl named Jeannie Singleton. As dawn was breaking in Kalamazoo, the amount of police officers from various departments throughout southern Michigan tripled, and the large groups of community volunteers were close to 1,000 in number.

Leading search teams this day were local and state police officers, the National Guard, Western Michigan College ROTC, and local Naval Reserves. The Civic Air Patrol continued to monitor with several planes in the air along with a National Guard helicopter.

Dorothy Singleton agreed to be interviewed for all the newspapers believing her pleas may aid in the return of her daughter. It was clearly obvious from Dorothy's anguished face that enduring the disappearance of her daughter were her worst nightmares come true. She remarked several times to the press that she just "felt numb," and described how on that first night she sat on the porch all night and prayed.

"Last night (the second night) I got a little bit of sleep, but the nights are the worst," Dorothy continued. "I can hold up in the daylight, but when it gets dark, I just can't take it."

Dorothy pleaded with the public that if someone had Jeannie to please allow her to come home. "If someone has my little girl I beg them to bring her back to me. I don't care who it is or why it happened. I don't care about anything anymore. I just want my little girl," she openly cried.

Steve Singleton took on a different tone from those first interviews. He came across as a man who felt the need to defend himself. Steve was quoted as saying "One of us was home while the other parent worked. Maybe we have to work too hard, but what can you do when you have to work hard to keep the family together."

The three older Singleton children, Mary, Patsy, and Jimmy, would join in the searches for their little sister; Steve and Chuck would stay home.

One reporter commented, "Stevie and Chucky are not aware of what all the excitement was about." After interviewing Steve ourselves for this book, it is obvious to us that this reporter was quite naïve about the impact this search was making on the young child. Steve very clearly comprehended what was happening.

One quote from Captain Riley Stewart, which we found in the Toledo Blade newspaper made us hope that despite giving interviews to the press, Jeannie's parents didn't actually read the newspapers. While the fear of Jeannie's safety was growing, Capt. Stewart said, "I think the chances that she is dead are much greater than those that she is alive."

Kalamazoo County Sheriff's Department pleaded with county farmers to check their fields as they would know their own land best and would have an easier time spotting something unusual. Authorities openly admitted that every square inch of land could not be searched, so this request was repeated several times publicly during the coming days.

Michigan State Police issued an alert to all mail carriers in Kalamazoo County to be on the lookout for Jeannie or anything suspicious.

The Kalamazoo Gazette posted an announcement that they would pay a reward of $500 for information leading to the arrest of "the person or persons responsible for the disappearance of Jeannie Singleton."

Arrangements were made in conjunction with FBI Agent Curran for the local police to intercept all mail coming to the Singleton household. Authorities would grab the mail when it was delivered; take it back to the station where every piece was opened and examined before being given to the parents. Regardless of the fact the parents obviously didn't make enough money to warrant asking for a ransom; police still had hopes of a ransom note or some taunting communication from the kidnapper.

Captain Stewart took charge of three officers and had them accompany him up the hill to the Kalamazoo's State Psychiatric Northwest Unit. Lingering theories of an asylum worker or an escaped mental patient had to be ruled out. The officers held a meeting with Harry Gildea, business manager for the sanitarium, in which they learned of John Stowe, a former patient. Twenty-two year old Stowe was released into convalescent care but was employed in the Food Service Department of the asylum. Stowe suffered from mental illness brought on by his emotional problems with sex. When the officers found out John Stowe worked at the asylum until 7:00pm that night, they immediately wrote him off as a suspect and never questioned him.

Mr. Gildea then reminded the officers that the institution also employed several ground keepers who were not current or former patients. Those men had indeed worked the grounds on May 23rd. After collecting the groundskeepers' names and addresses, the officers left the premises satisfied that the kidnapper was not one of the insane patients. There was no mention in the case files given to us by the police of any questioning of these groundskeepers.

During the day a call came into the Kalamazoo Police Department from a Mr. James Vlien, a six-year friend of the Singleton family who resided on James Street. Mr. Vlien agreed to come down to the station and give his statement directly to Capt. Stewart. According to Vlien, on the evening of May 23rd, he spotted Jeannie walking hand-in-hand with two other young girls in Upjohn Park around 6:10pm. While he gave a brief description of the two other girls he was positive the third girl was Jeannie. While writing out his statement, another officer talked with residents around the Upjohn Pharmaceutical Company and learned the identities of the two unknown girls. These little girls gave the name of the third child with them that day. The girl was June Barnhart, age 9. When police returned to the station and gave these names and details to Mr. Vlien, the man was insistent these were not the girls he saw in the park that sunny Monday evening.

Capt. Stewart traveled to the Singleton home and inquired if the couple had any friends around the Crosstown Parkway area. While they gave the names of two families, they quickly stated that both families only have male children.

Regardless of suspecting this could be a waste of time, Capt. Stewart still wrote down the names of the two families and paid them a visit. He was correct in his assumption. Not only did the two households have only male children, but the boys also didn't know of any girls around Jeannie's age that lived in the nearby neighborhoods. Returning back to his office he couldn't shake the thought of how Mr. Vlien was so positive about his identity of Jeannie, but yet no young girls have come forward to claim they were with the missing girl on that day.

A local citizen came forward to testify he noticed something of interest on the day Jeannie disappeared. Ronnie Roeder stated when he got out of work from the Kalamazoo Stationary Company he was driving near the intersection of Ravine and Douglas when he noticed an unknown male stop his car just south of the gas station and was lean out the window to talk to two young girls. He mentioned both girls walked away, but the brief encounter gave Mr. Roeder and uneasy feeling. The car was described as a dark blue '53 or '54 Chevy, and the man inside looked to be approximately 40 years of age, light complexion and wearing glasses. This would be the first of many mentions about a dark blue or green car cruising that particular neighborhood in the days surrounding Jeannie's disappearance.

A list of men, who were deemed sexual deviants, was included with the Singleton case files we obtained we were shocked to discover portions of the list included homosexual men. These gentlemen never committed any criminal offenses, but here they were on a list of deviants as if they were already guilty of heinous wrongdoings. Many of these "suspects" were going about their lives and doing nothing wrong, but their sexual orientation made them an instant target for the detectives.

With this derogatory list in hand, the Kalamazoo Police initiated the beginning stages of rounding up all known sex offenders throughout the city. Some of the people were in the midst of their employment when they were approached, handcuffed and led away in front of their coworkers for nothing more than questioning. I am sure several of them probably lost their positions when business owners learned of their criminal backgrounds and didn't want to employ a person of ill-repute in their business.

One such person was Jerry M. Noble, a 17-year-old was in the middle of his job as a busboy at the Burdick Hotel when police arrived, handcuffed the young man in front of his co-workers, and was led away. This was just one example of the "sexual deviant roundups" local and county law enforcement engaged in immediately after the disappearance of Jeannie.

Noble came under police radar when it was discovered he not only had three previous run-ins with molestation and indecent liberties when he was 15, but he once dated one of the older Singleton sisters. It was found that Noble was very friendly with the Singleton family and had been to their house on many occasions.

During their investigation, Noble gave conflicting stories as to his whereabouts on May 23rd. In fact, the young man gave so many different versions that it became difficult for police to check out his statements; each detective was given a different version of events. In hopes Noble would finally give some credible answers, officials decided to keep him in jail overnight.

On day two Noble decided he spent enough time being incarcerated and told detectives he was at the Michigan Theater from 3pm – 8pm that Monday afternoon. Exhausted by the fact this statement could be yet again another lie; Noble was transported to the Michigan State Police Post in Paw Paw and subjected to a lie detector test.

The test proved that the young man was finally telling the truth and had no connection to the Jeannie Singleton disappearance. He was later released from police custody and officially cleared. Unfortunately, the local newspapers had already picked up the tip about a person in custody. I am sure his employer, the Burdick Hotel, was less than pleased about his on-site arrest and his neighbors in the 400 block of South Park probably kept a close eye on this not-to-be-trusted young man after his return home.

While working on the Singleton case, Kalamazoo Police were contacted by a concerned father who stated a young boy named John Wilkins should be investigated. This gentleman was the parent of a 4 ½-year-old daughter who Wilkins had molested only two weeks prior to Jeannie's disappearance.

14-year-old Wilkins was brought to the police station for questioning; his mother following close behind them. When questioned about his whereabouts on May 23rd, Wilkins commented that he had been home all day. When his mother was questioned at length about the same day she stated that he was home all day except for a short period of time at 5:00pm when, ironically, he told his mother he had joined in the search for Jeannie. The mother claimed he returned home about an hour later.

This lack of a timeline and the irony of this young man's whereabouts, according to his mother, did not go unnoticed by the investigators. They decided to shift gears and push for more information in regards to the alleged molestation of the 4-year old girl instead.

Wilkin did admit he had invited the little girl back to his mother's upstairs apartment on W. North Street while his mother was at work. In fact, Wilkins testified that he "carried" the child up to his mother's apartment. While there the two merely watched TV together, and when the girl had to go to the bathroom, he did not follow her in.

Statements obtained from the Juvenile Court contained a much darker version of this innocent afternoon. The child mentioned that when she entered the bathroom, Wilkins joined her, took down the girl's pants and performed cunnilingus on her. When asked about the sexually explicit material found in his bedroom Wilkins admitted that he possessed pornographic photos, books, and illustrations he had personally drawn and used those materials for self-stimulation.

Investigators knew Wilkins wasn't completely truthful, so a lie-detector test was administered with the approval of his mother. His results highlighted deception of the critical questions about the 4-year-old girl.

Wilkins was released back into this mother's custody. As the case in regards to the little girl was already pending in Juvenile Court, no new charges could be filed, but the results of the test were forwarded on to the prosecutor. In the official police statement on May 31, 1955, detectives placed the following conclusion on record; "We are thoroughly convinced that John Wilkins is guilty of the offense with the 4-year-old girl, but we can voice no opinion on the Singleton incident. We are of the opinion, however, that he would be capable."

Young Mr. Wilkins may have been more than capable of committing a horrible act on Jeannie, but the evidence just wasn't there. Within the next 48 hours, police took the teenager off the suspect list.

As the afternoon dragged into the evening, it became apparent that Mother Nature decided to become uncooperative with search and rescue teams. Strong winds, heavy rains, and fog hampered the investigation. This was especially true for the aircraft. Visibility in valleys was so low that it would be impossible to see the ground through the dense fog. Tornado warnings rang through the newswire constantly throughout the evening and into the night. It was mentioned in one newspaper that one helicopter almost crashed when a strong gust of wind suddenly appeared. Thankfully, the skilled pilot was able to quickly regain control but it was apparently all aerial searches would have to cease until the winds died down.

The ground teams were more determined than ever to find the missing child. Fearing the girl may perish from exposure from the weather elements people worked tirelessly through fields of overgrown brush, wooded areas, and abandoned buildings.

Excitement ran through the police department when their first lead was finally brought in from a search crew. Earlier in the day, shortly before the skies opened up, searchers found a pink kerchief/ribbon was found hanging from a small low tree branch in the Kleinstruck Preserve Area, approximately three miles away from the Singleton home.

The police immediately noted the kerchief was dry, which suggested it had not been hanging there during the night when it rained.

The kerchief was taken to the Singleton home where both Dorothy and Patsy stated it as the one Jeannie may have worn to school that fateful Monday. Armed with this positive information, detectives gathered hair samples from Jeannie's hairbrush and a knitted hat she often wore and sent them to the Michigan Crime Laboratory to be analyzed against strands of hair found wrapped in the ribbon.

The next day, the results of the hair samples came back to Captain Stewart. The hair taken from the brush was similar to the hair found wrapped in the pink ribbon; while the hair that was taken from the knitted hat was not a match at all. Though confused as to why the hair from the cap didn't match the hair from the ribbon, this piece of information was still considered the best lead they had so far.

Two items that were found during searches did peak the detectives' interests. A blue blanket, found in a car belonging to William Birkhold, 128 E. Dutton St., had stains that tested positive for blood. A girl's flowered handkerchief, which held stains that were also positive for blood, was discovered on state property located at the west end of Center Street. Nothing was noted in the case files pertaining further to these two bloodied articles. We do know through our research that these items had ultimately no connection to Jeannie's case, but it would be interesting to discover if they were evidence of another unknown crime.

By the end of this day, police had received more than 500 tips; all proving to be completely worthless. With no word from Jeannie, authorities, reporters and Kalamazoo citizens all began to suspect the worse. They feared Jeannie had become the victim of a dangerous sexual predator. These thoughts swirled in their minds, but everyone was careful not to voice their suspicions in front of the Singletons.

The heavy rains continued, the wind blew stronger, and Dorothy Singleton spent a third cold night on her front porch, praying to see her little girl run up the street and dive into her loving arms.

May 26, 1955

Two days after Jeannie's abduction, three teenagers waiting for their morning class to begin at Central High heard a shocking statement given by 16-year-old Don DeYoung to some of his buddies. While discussing the Singleton disappearance Don declared "They will find the girl in Allegan Forest because that's where I had left her."

Concerned this young man may be telling the truth, Beverly Davis called the police when she returned home later that afternoon.

Police waited for DeYoung to return home from his job at Hart's Grocery Store at 7:00pm. It was then that he was confronted about his earlier statement. A nervous DeYoung stated that he was just fooling around amongst friends, but never denied he made that exact statement. The young man claimed that on May 23rd he had come home from school around 4:00pm then immediately left for his grocery store job and worked his normal 3-hour shift. After arriving home from work, he ate supper with his family changed clothes and traveled to Vicksburg with a friend until 9:00pm that night.

Before the police left the DeYoung residence, they confiscated the clothing worn two days prior by the teenager for laboratory analysis.

Everything the young man told police checked out. When the officer returned back to the DeYoung residence, the boy got a stern lecture from not only the officer but also his father about the dangers of messing around and not censoring what you say in front of others. Let's hope Don DeYoung learned to never joke about anything like this again!

Investigating officers were extremely busy on this day tracking down dozens of tips that poured into the police station. Officer McCarty was given the task of checking out a man deemed a "sexual psychopath" who was released from the Ionia State Hospital nine months before Jeannie's disappearance.

Hugh Penn was arrested in May of 1952 on charges of indecent exposure. What he had done to receive this charge was a bit more severe than simple exposure. He had grabbed a young girl by the breast while having his penis out at the same time. Penn confessed to this and many similar violations against other girls and women throughout the city. Regardless of how many victims failed to report the attacks he finally found one who wouldn't stay silent. He was convicted and sent to the mental hospital in July of that year.

Having been released from the hospital, Penn was living in Kalamazoo at the Y.M.C.A. in room #325. He was sleeping in his room when Officer DeYoung arrived. Upon questioning the groggy convict, he was informed that he was currently on parole. In the 1950s a person could be paroled and be monitored by churches and other religious organizations.

Rev. Herman DeHune of the New Apostolic Church agreed to take Penn on in this respect. When questioned about the Singleton family, he admitted to having met the Singleton parents at Rev. DeHune's residence, since they were parishioners at the church, but didn't recall any of the Singleton children and had no knowledge of where the Singletons resided.

While being interviewed, he informed officers that after being paroled he had gone from job to job until he finally managed to secure two part-time employment positions, one being at Aden's Cleaners on Portage Road. When the date of May 23rd was brought up by Officer DeYoung, Penn stated he went to Aden's Cleaners around 2:00pm that afternoon since one of the regular delivery drivers was on vacation. When he arrived at his place of employment, he found that Mr. Aden wasn't there. He hung around the establishment and waited for his boss to arrive which, according to Penn, didn't occur until 5:00pm. According to Penn after his boss arrived the two went next door for a root beer.

When questioning the owner, another timeline of events was given. According to Mr. Aden, he had arrived at the business around 2:00pm and found his employee waiting for him. After discussing a delivery he wanted Penn to make, they went next door for a root beer. Mr. Aden specified he was positive they were back in the shop around 2:30pm and Penn left to make a delivery on Ada Street.

Later in the evening, a report came in that two men were seen carrying a body between them into the field across from 3707 E. Main Street. Upon arrival, police found three cars alongside the road with one of them being the green Chevrolet Tudor that the witness stated was the car these men carried the body out of. The car was registered to Joseph Doguay who resided on Ball Street.

Shortly after the police arrived at the field; scores of firemen, National Guard, Civil Air Patrol and the Township Police arrived and began a search of the field. After an hour, two unknown men walked out of the field and were quickly corralled by the police and brought to the police station for questioning.

Both men claimed they had decided to search for Jeannie. Officers checked the men out and called their wives. Both wives confirmed the men wanted to help with the search. The witness's claim of seeing a "body bag" carrying by them was never resolved. No large bundles could be found, and both men denied carrying anything into the field. The men were released two hours later and were cleared of involvement.

Back at the Singleton residence, Detective Aldrich was learning about the man the family believes may have harmed their daughter. The reason for that fear follows.

In the latter part of 1950 Dorothy's half-sister, Orpha Case was living at the Singleton home. When it became obvious to all that Dorothy's 14-year-old sibling was pregnant, the family demanded answers and Orpha refused to divulge the name of the baby's father and began telling a long trek of lies.

Not knowing what else to do Dorothy contacted the authorities. Policewoman Timmis questioned Orpha, but the girl steadfastly refused to give up any information. Orpha was placed in a Detention Home for being non-compliant for police, and everyone involved hoped this move would scare the teenager enough to confess. After three days of confinement, the girl broke down in sobs and spilled out the real truth.

In the spring of 1950, Orpha began work as a babysitter for the Streeter Family who resided on Portage Road in Kalamazoo. The married 24-year-old father of two, Eugene, was working for DeNooyers Chevrolet Company in Battle Creek. He was attracted to the babysitter and began a torrid affair with the minor. Orpha admitted that sex occurred multiple times in Eugene's car that spring and summer.

A warrant was issued for his arrest charging him with "bastardy," and he was promptly brought back to Michigan from Fort Wayne, Indiana. Once authorities had Streeter locked up, the bastardy charge was quickly replaced with the more serious charge of statutory rape.

Although the pregnancy was obvious evidence of a sexual affair, Street pled not guilty to the charge and continued his denial all the way through court. His testimony fell on deaf ears and on October 30, 1950, he was found guilty of statutory rape and was given a sentence of 1 ½ to 10 years at the Michigan Reformatory in Ionia. Court records indicated he was paroled on March 25th, 1952 and was living with his wife Lucille in Delton, Michigan.

Dorothy and Steve Singleton pled with the detectives to tread lightly with the investigation of Eugene Streeter as they have heard whispers for years that he was still very bitter about their involvement in his conviction. If Streeter had nothing to do with Jeannie disappearance as revenge against their family, they were fearful he would become angry enough to cause harm after he was interrogated. Detective Aldrich assured the parents he would conduct a very quiet investigation and make no mention of their conversation to him.

After obtaining a current address for the Streeter Family, Sheriff Donovan from Hickory Corners recalled that Streeter was arrested on

May 7th, 1955 east of Delton, Michigan for reckless driving and was injured.

Along with Deputy Sheriff Ivan Smith from Delton, the two men ventured over to the Streeter household to have a talk with either Eugene or his wife. Mrs. Streeter was home with her four children and allowed the detectives inside to speak with her about Eugene. Lucille informed the detectives that Eugene had destroyed his car and was unable to return to work due to a severe knee injury he suffered in the crash.

Upon asking about May 23rd, Mrs. Streeter said her husband had been with her that Monday and helped with the children as she was once again pregnant. On Tuesday, Eugene now drove an old Chevrolet half-ton truck and had traveled to Battle Creek to deal with an insurance issue stemming from pending medical bills.

When the conversation moved along to the subject of her husband's incarceration, she readily admitted that Eugene had been very bitter after his return home but has since "nearly gotten over it." She mentioned that when she and her husband had heard the news, they wondered if Jeannie had any relation to the Singleton family Orpha was staying within 1950.

The detectives surprised her further by confirming they were all talking about the same family and inquired if she thought Eugene was bitter enough to have had any involvement with Jeannie's abduction. The wife stressed very forcefully that if she has any doubt her husband had something to do with the little girl's disappearance, she would turn him in immediately as to protect her other children. She gave her opinion that only an insane person would do something like that. She did, however, promise to contact Sheriff Smith is she finds out differently.

After talking with his wife and then spotting Eugene at the Gilkey Lake Tavern hobbling around horrendously despite the aid of crutches, both men felt Eugene Streeter could not have successfully hobbled around and abducted Jeannie on that day. In addition to this, there were no eyewitness reports of an old noisy brown truck in or around the neighborhood last Monday. Back in his car Detective Aldrich relaxed his head back and closed his eyes, feeling the waves of overwhelming disappointment of another lead gone.

Other promising leads came into the police station on this day:

Two workers at the Fish Hatchery were overheard discussing their extra-marital fun when one gentleman boasted that on Monday, while his wife was in Texas, he picked up 'some strange stuff." His coworker promptly told him not to talk about this out loud, but it was too late — an acquaintance heard the statement and went to the police by the end of the day. Upon further investigation by the Michigan State Police, they learned neither gentleman had been near the Blakeslee neighborhood on that day and wasn't even aware a little girl had been abducted in Kalamazoo.

A woman by the name of Pearl Garber stated that a man by the name of Charles Shingledecker had been charged with rape several years ago and had returned back to Kalamazoo to work as a watchman for the Pennsylvania Railroad on East Walnut Street. Officers became confused when they could not locate a criminal record for Mr. Shingledecker, and his employer stated he has worked for the railroad for many years; not a recent hire. Further questioning of Ms. Garber was unsuccessful. The great rumor mill of Kalamazoo was responsible for putting an end to this lead — police learned that Mr. Shingledecker was, in fact, one of Ms. Garber's past husbands. In fact, she deemed all of her former spouses to be sexual deviants.

Police responded to a call for a detective to assist with a search party in the 1600 block of West North Street. After arrival, it was discovered the search party was holding a teenager by the name of Richard Starner. Starner, slightly mentally retarded, was found wandering in a field between Blakeslee, West North, and Hilbert Streets. This young patient had ventured away from the nearby TB hospital and citizens within the search party were sure Starner had something to do with Jeannie's disappearance. After returning Starner to the hospital, the police learned that he was confined on Monday and only wandered outside today because he could see the searchers in the distance and became intrigued.

A call came into the Paw Paw State Police Post about a suspicious gentleman that was seen hitchhiking north on Douglas Avenue at Mossell Avenue on Monday. He was identified as Emil Peterson, age 38, from Sault Saint Marie. He proved to be an escapee from the Veteran's Hospital in Battle Creek. After questioning Mr. Peterson, it was concluded the man had nothing to do with the case and unfortunately was not an eyewitness to any of the events. He was promptly returned to the VA Hospital.

A total of 23 men were brought in, arrested and taken to various police stations on this day for lie detector tests. None of these gentlemen were spotted in the Blakeslee neighborhood nor was a random tip called in regards to them. This was another "round up" of either known homosexuals or men who decided to cheat on their wives with younger teenage girls.

A report came in from bus driver Neal Fleugal that a female passenger had told him of a young boy, either 8 or 9 years old, who had reported that he had seen Jeannie Singleton get into a car at Douglas and North Streets after school on May 23rd. Police found the boy to be Charles Miller, age 10, who lived by the gravel pits.

His tale in regards to his observations of this day turned muddled very quickly. The boy stating that he saw her being picked up at the corner mentioned, but she was let out of the car at the corner of Blakeslee and Douglas, only to be picked up by the same car further up the hill on Blakeslee. The police swiftly concluded the child's observations of that day should be discounted. It is possible that it is once again Charles who also appears later in case files. This mention is about a young boy who claimed to have walked home with Jeannie whose statement seemed to be "Imaginary and flights of fantasy."

Detective McCarty was instructed to check out George Henschel of 1207 Ogden Avenue. Police were informed word-of-mouth that Henschel had been previously mixed up in some kind of sexual offense in the past. Arriving at the residence, he talked with Henschel and learned that the man had been sick for quite some time but did walk down to Tarnow's Dairy to purchase some milk on Monday but haven't left the house since. When McCarty asked both Henschel and his sister Mary if he could come in and search the house the detective was startled by the fierce refusal that followed. Henschel firmly stated the detective "Will not find that little girl's body in our house!"

When McCarty pushed the issue with both residents, threatening them with official city involvement, both parties reluctantly agreed to a search of the home. Detective McCarty's report described the conditions of the house as "Indescribable and would have to be seen before it could be believed." The officer had walked into a classic hoarder's house - packed to the ceiling with boxes, clothes, tin cans and garbage on every level of the home from the basement to the attic. Only a one-foot wide path was visible to certain parts of the house while other areas clearly hadn't been accessed for months or even years. McCarty agreed silently with Henschel about not finding a little girl's body in this house and couldn't wait to leave the smelly premises.

Some leads came in by way of letters with some letters capturing more attention than others. One such letter was dated May 28th, 1955 from a Harry Armstrong of Flushing Michigan and was addressed to the Chief of Detectives of the Kalamazoo Police Department. Armstrong was a believer of the spiritual world and wanted to inform the detectives of the group's visit by Jeannie. The letter follows in its entirety.

> "My name is Harry Armstrong of Flushing, Michigan. I am a member of the Spiritualist Church in Flint, Michigan. My purpose is one of information, in sending you this letter. During the time a medium was in a trance, the following events took place:
>
> Jeannie Shingleton (sic) came through and stated before she was kidnapped and slain, she was sitting on a curb when a man

drove along in a car and asked her what the matter was.
Jeannie replied she was tired. The man asked her to get into his
car, and he would buy her some ice cream, and then take her
home. The girl got into the car, but the man did not take her
home instead he took her out into the country and choked her to
death. The body is in woods, in a shallow grave, a short distance
north of your city. This man's name is Horace Greude, age 45,
divorced from his wife, whose name is Beatrice, he has a little
daughter, age 8. This man originally came from Pennsylvania to
Lima, Ohio. He was employed as a postman in Lima. Is described
as a broad-shouldered man wearing a blue zipper jacket, brown
pants, white dress shirt, open at the neck, well-kept hands, and
has a signet ring on his right hand with the initial 'H" on it. His
car is a 1952 Buick Sedan, Ohio license number CE-5413. The car
has a red and green plaid blanket on the back seat. There is a
gray felt hat sitting in the back window. This man was en route
to Benton Harbor. This is the man that killed Jeannie Shingleton.
The above facts were given to us by Jeannie Shingleton, to be
sent to you to help apprehend her killer.

I would appreciate it if you would advise me if any of this
information checks out.

Sincerely, Harry Armstrong, Flushing, Michigan"

Detective Sgt. Beck of the Paw Paw State Police Post called the Flint
Police to obtain more information about Armstrong. It turns out that
Harry Armstrong was a Deputy in the Genesee County Sheriff's
Department and that he belonged to the Spiritualist Church. Det. Beck
stated that during his phone conversation with Deputy Armstrong, the
man seemed reputable and very convincing. Armstrong did make one
correction though. He said he was mistaken about the license plate; it
was a Michigan plate, not an Ohio one. Before ending the call, Deputy
Armstrong's last message to convey was that Jeannie's body would be
found in 4 days and approximately 15 miles north of Kalamazoo.

While some of the officers may have chalked up this correspondence to a flaky psychic thinking they could actually help out, Steve Singleton took it to heart. Unless you have stepped into the same shoes as Dorothy and Steve Singleton, you will never know the true anguish these parents were going through. To stay home, day after day and not hearing your daughter walk through that door at night had to be a new version of Hell on Earth.

We would never be able to sit at home and wait for word if one of our children were missing. I would venture to say that you wouldn't have been able to hold either of us back. I am sure Steve Singleton felt something similar and had an inner need to join in the search for his daughter; even if he had to go it alone.

After hearing the "tip" from the Spiritualist Church, he began to drive around the country areas north of Kalamazoo in hopes of spotting Jeannie. Since he didn't keep track of his locations during these periods of absence, unfortunately, many citizens misconstrued Steve's efforts and began to wonder if he may have had something to do with his daughter's demise. This is a misconception that would haunt the investigation for decades.

May 27, 1955

Officials soon hoped the long Memorial Day weekend may spur more search volunteers or perhaps cause vacationers to be more observant of any lakefront properties.

Chief Heywood's statements were repeated in many newspapers throughout Michigan, urging people to keep close watch of the waters and shorelines. He additionally reminded nature lovers to look under piles of brushes and down ravines if hiking through the woods. His indirect meaning was not lost upon the Kalamazoo Gazette reporter who inquired as to a slightly different tone when talking about searching for little Jeannie.

Hanging his head low for a moment and collecting his thoughts, Heywood raised his head and stated for the press and public, "We have given up hope that the child is alive and would remind searchers that it is a body for which they are looking- a body which may be cramped into a small enclosure or might be hidden by a small thicket or bush."

With this statement now verbalized Captain Stewart wanted to inform the public of what procedures to adhere to if they should stumble upon Jeannie's body. Procedures such as not touching the body, and not to pick up or move any objects on the ground surrounding the body, either call the police yourself or have someone else perform this task without causing alarm to the public, keep any passersby away from the area and stay with the victim until authorities arrive.

When the Gazette was distributed later that day the unimaginable possibility was now forefront in everyone's minds – Jeannie Singleton was probably dead. Hope can be powerful but at some point, no matter what the circumstance; reality has a way of slamming down. Hundreds of volunteers would continue the search despite the chance of an ominous outcome.

Not long after the newspapers hit the stands, a large cloudburst hit the city with heavy rains, dimming hope of finding evidence which might help lead to the discovery of Jeannie. By this time the young girl had been missing for five days, and leads were starting to slow down for the girl citizens' had deemed "Vanished into thin air."

While family and friends had images of a cold, hurt and scared little girl suffering yet another day in the elements, the police had an entirely different image in mind - evidence of murder was being washed away in these storms.

The Civil Air Patrol, who up until this time had been initiating foot searches, changed its tactics. Tagged with the name "Operation Flat Top," 20 volunteered truck owners performed road-by-road searches throughout Kalamazoo County. The National Guard, by request of Governor Philip Hart, was to continue searches with the use of vehicles and various equipment needs.

The reward for Jeannie, with the first $500 initiated by the Kalamazoo Gazette, now grew to $1,500 which was a substantial amount in 1955. Donations had poured in with the hopes that someone who had information would want the money bad enough to give up information on a friend or loved one. While the reward money was greatly appreciated by the Singleton family, it caused the Kalamazoo Police Department to spend many wasted hours on false leads and sometimes outrageous claims pouring in from locals attempting any means they could to obtain the reward

During the holiday weekend, Chief Heywood received a call from Dorothy Singleton stating that a blind woman who resided at 2526 Willow Blvd. may have information regarding this case.

Officer Kincaid arrived at the provided address and spoke with Donna Hall, the blind woman mentioned in the phone conversation. Ms. Hall informed the officer that in the early morning hours of Sunday morning, May 29th, she heard a car come from the south on Willis Street, turn on to Willow Street and stop in front of her home. Thinking someone was approaching the house, she waited to hear the sounds of someone opening her front gate.

When not a sound was to be heard she got up to move to the front door when she heard a loud splash from the direction of the Kalamazoo River followed by the sound of a vehicle trunk being closed. Shortly following was the sound of a car door being closed, the vehicle starting up and driving off veering west on Willow Street.

When Officer Kincaid walked back to his patrol vehicle, he noticed neighbor Peter Baker and questioned the man about any disturbances he heard at 2:00am as well. Mr. Baker claimed to not hear a single thing but did inform the officer that it was not uncommon for partiers to be in the vicinity and people would occasionally stop on Willow to throw bags of trash into the river. Mr. Baker also entertained the officer with a mutual theory from the neighborhood that Ms. Hall was nuts; always talking about UFO sightings around her house and trying to find some way to get her name into the newspapers.

Accompanied by Officer Conroy both men went to the river bank and was not surprised to find not a single indication anything was amiss near the river bank. Just to be cautious though he did have Captain Stewart arrange for the Fire Department to initiate a water search near the vicinity of the shoreline at Willow Street. For good measure the Fire Department brought in grappling hooks to drag the bottom of the river; nothing was found other than trash.

By the end of the day on May 30th news soon spread that the FBI had determined the Singleton case lacked proof of federal violation. There continued to be no evidence to support Jeannie may have been taken across state lines after her abduction.

Special Agent Fred McIntire reminded the public the FBI would remain in close contact with local authorities should any indications of a federal violation presents itself. In addition to this Agent, McIntire stated the FBI "Would make their facilities, such as the identification bureau, laboratories and the missing person's notifications, available to local law enforcement but the FBI cannot take an active role in the investigation."

Kalamazoo detectives returned to the Singleton home to re-interview all family members and have their testimonies recorded. Authorities had hoped that perhaps some memory might have triggered during this now week-long ordeal. The family readily complied with the officers. They would do anything to help locate their beloved family member. From the statements enclosed with the Singleton Case Files we obtained, it appears no new tips came from recording these statements. The memories of all family members matched the verbal statements given to the police after the abduction.

We mentioned that Steve Singleton's personal quest to locate his daughter made many citizens suspicious of his involvement. At some unspecified date, the father received a "confidential report" that Jeannie may be located in a building near Cuttlerville about five miles southeast of Grand Rapids. His obsession over a certain shack caused authorities to accompany him on three separate trips to perform a thorough search of the property, but nothing was ever found. This behavior created many whispers in their city that perhaps Steve knew something about the abduction of his little girl. This misconception still holds true for surviving Kalamazoo locals, we have been told by many that people believed Steve Singleton killed his daughter. Personally, we feel he was a man so desperate to find his little girl that he would believe almost anything, and do almost anything to find her. He didn't care what people thought of his actions and theories he just wanted his daughter back home.

Eight days into the disappearance of Jeannie Singleton several things began to change; search parties consisted of fewer and fewer people, the National Guard was taken off of active searching and placed on standby, and lastly, the Singleton parents decided to return to their employment duties. The grieving parents shared with police they believed Jeannie would not be found alive and living for the rest of the family needed to go on.

Unfortunately, their nightmarish world would be rocked the following day again.

Units from multiple branches of the military aided in the search for Jeannie
Photo courtesy of MLive Media Group, Kalamazoo Gazette, and WMU archives.

Hundreds of volunteers helped to search for Jeannie.
Photo courtesy of MLive Media Group, Kalamazoo Gazette, and WMU archives.

Pink kerchief found in the Kleinstuck Preserve is examined by the family.
Photo courtesy of MLive Media Group, Kalamazoo Gazette, and WMU archives.

PSYCHOLOGY OF AN ABDUCTEE'S FAMILY

Unless you have experienced the nightmare of your child being abducted, you will never begin to imagine the emotions Steve and Dorothy faced. When May 24th came and went with no word or sign of their daughter Jeannie, the threads of hope began to unravel, and a new reality had to be faced. They may never see their child again.

The family members and friends that are left behind after abduction go through different levels of shock and disbelief. Pre-stressors that were already present in a marriage will be added to the new-found stress causing some couples, no matter how loving their marriage is, to break apart. They often start to blame one another, and sometimes these feelings can escalate into domestic violence.

When a child is not returned quickly, parents then face a multitude of new choices. Do they go back to work? If one parent does not work, how will the bills be paid? They wonder when, if ever, they will see their child again.

Some parents will cling to their faith while others will have a sense of abandonment and will blame "God" for taking their child away. Some will find solace in alcohol or an illegal substance. This often unknowingly causes the other spouse to either distance themselves more or forces them to become caretaker of the inebriated adult. This will continue to add stress to an already unimaginable situation.

Time does not heal all wounds. The entire family is left in a state of limbo. Families need answers. Until a child's whereabouts are known, and a reunion has occurred, a family cannot move on with a normal life. The parents wonder how they can possibly be happy again when they do not know the location of their child or if their child is dead or alive. Knowing your child might be experiencing terror and pain makes any parent feel like the most helpless soul on Earth.

The siblings of an abducted child go through their own emotional rollercoaster and often become forgotten victims. They have not only lost their sibling, but in a sense, they have lost their parents too. Searching parents are so focused on their missing child they have a tendency, without meaning to; to forget about the existing children and their needs. The youngest of the siblings will often experience nightmares of the perpetrator returning to the home and taking one of them. Occasionally the older siblings can have feelings of resentment towards their parents as the older children are forced to take the role of the parents and care for the younger children in the home. They too feel their lives were ripped away from them when the abduction occurred.

While everyone wishes for a happy ending, the truth is that the lives of abducted children and their families are forever changed.

Steve remained active in the searches for Jeannie while Dorothy granted the press interviews and made public pleas for Jeannie's safe return. Dorothy became Jeannie's biggest public advocate; never hiding her anguish from the public, showing pictures of Jeannie to the press at every given opportunity, and begging the perpetrator to just bring back her little girl.

Steve and Dorothy tried to keep the family intact and find normalcy when it was possible. While eventually, the siblings found comfort in daily routine, Steve and Dorothy had to force themselves to eat, rest, and stay strong. Sleep became a rare event as they were seldom granted a reprieve from the horrible images and nightmares when they closed their eyes.

Friends and family gathered at the Singleton house daily to offer comfort, helping with Jeannie's siblings, and learn of any news from the detectives. Steve, being the father, became encompassed by guilt and anger not only toward the monster who took her little girl, but angry at himself for failing to protect her. Life for Dorothy would likely have been more emotionally difficult than it was for Steve. She would internalize more of the despair for the sake of their children. It's the concept of "if Mom falls apart, we all fall apart." Mothers have to remain the matriarch of the family regardless of how numb they may feel inside; Dorothy wasn't any different.

The dark days continued, and the emotional strains began to chip away at their souls. As the days grew longer, one goal remained with the Singleton family. They wanted Jeannie home; one way or another.

Steve and **Dorothy Singleton seek counsel from their minister.**
Photo courtesy of MLive Media Group & the Kalamazoo Gazette

A GAME OF HIDE & SEEK

On June 1st let me take you approximately 18 miles away from the grieving Singleton Family, struggling to survive on Blakeslee Street. The day started out beautiful and sunny, so beautiful in fact that five children eagerly ran outside to play in this remote corner of Allegan County named Doster.

The Prolo family had three children Owen (age 13), Maggie (age 10) and Jerry (age 5) and would normally be found playing with their niece and nephew, Virginia (age 7) and Billy (age 5). Hide and Seek was their favorite outdoor game to play in their private outdoor playground, a large grove of white pine neatly arranged in rows.

Jerry remembers to this day the field of pines was a "fun place to play where they sometimes built forts in the trees." The children played there almost daily when the weather allowed. This day was no exception, and the children prepared their game by traveling to the "starting point," the clearing at the top of the hill just north of the house. Owen, not interested in playing the childish game with the rest of the kids, decided to explore on his own throughout the property.

An hour later the eldest Prolo child emerged from the pine trees and ran towards the children. The surviving Prolo children described Owen looking "pale and scared" as he walked towards them and then announced he thought he found a dead girl. The group of children laughed believing Owen was once again trying to trick them. Rather defiantly he demanded that the children come to see for themselves if they don't believe him.

The children followed Owen as he explained to his playmates how he was running through the pines and nearly tripped over the victim's feet. Billy recalls to this day all the children were scared as they followed the older child. They didn't know what to expect, and the thought Owen was telling the truth was even more frightening.

Owen abruptly stopped and pointed to an area between the trees. The children gathered around and saw what appeared to be two feet, still wearing sandals and socks. Thinking the kids wanted a better view, Owen lifted up a low-hanging branch to present the rest of the gruesome picture, a decomposing body.

The girls shrieked and the children high-tailed it back to their house as fast as their young legs could carry them. Jerry recalls being the slowest kid in the group and tugging on Billy as they ran. Soon Billy was tugging at Jerry, each trying to gain more speed to reach the safety of home.

Owen reached the house first and promptly told his mother Pearl about finding the "dead girl." Thinking the children probably found a dead animal in the woods, the remaining children were told to stay with her at the house while her daughter-in-law Velma was escorted by Maggie to the location of this body.

Pushing back the branches the woman was shocked to see the bare legs and colorful sandals lying motionless amongst the pine needles. Both females quickly returned back to the house to inform Pearl that the children did indeed stumble upon a dead body.

The Prolo family was not wealthy by any means. The households could not afford a television, and the radio was used sporadically and only allowed by the adults. It's unknown if anyone in either household knew of Jennie Singleton's abduction. Since the family did not have a telephone, Velma and Owen ran a mile to the nearest neighbor to call the police.

At approximately 5:30pm, Kalamazoo detectives were alerted about a phone call from a woman in Doster claiming her kids just found the body of a young girl. Glancing at each other all the officers held the same thought. Jeannie had finally been found.

Prolo children receive the reward for discovering Jeannie

Photo courtesy of MLive Media Group, Kalamazoo Gazette, and WMU archives.

THE PINE GROVE

Quickly gathering auxiliary lights, ropes, and crime scene equipment Captain Stewart and Officers Kincaid, McCarty, Fox, and Jenkins raced to the small town of Doster.

Upon arriving at the scene, they were greeted by many Allegan County law enforcement officials, crime scene technicians, Allegan County's Prosecuting Attorney Dwight Cheever and Kalamazoo County's Prosecutor Jacob Dalm as well as Kalamazoo's Assistant Prosecutor Douglas Cook. The area was immediately roped off and guarded by Allegan County Officers. Several members of the Press were present but thankfully very cooperative about not intruding into the sealed off area.

When Medical Examiner Clyde Dickinson arrived, he was led to the body in the company of the remaining Kalamazoo officers. Any officer can tell you that no matter how many dead bodies they witness through the span of their careers it's never easy to view the body of a murdered child. One detective was quoted as saying "It eats at your soul and reminds you that heinous monsters do exist."

Jeannie was found lying face-down with the right side of her head on the ground with her arms outstretched with her left hand near her head. The right arm was more decomposed than the left. The left leg was partially concealed under a tree while the right leg was more exposed to the open area between the trees,

The body was clothed in multi-colored sandals, white socks, a slip and a pink plaid dress that was now pushed up above the girl's waist. Her panties were removed and partially lying under her right temple. The child's hair was in a pony-tail with a red rubber band.

Bruise marks were found on her right thigh, and it was obvious from a depression in the ground underneath her that weight was pressed on top of her. A broken branch from one of the pine trees was found partially under the victim's head, damp with blood and fluid from the head.

Two attendants arrived from the Truesdale Funeral Home to collect and transport the body. When they rolled the victim over, detectives noted maggot infestation surrounding the face and private areas. The dress was bunched up past the waist on the front as well, and the exposed skin was covered in insect bites.

The body was wrapped in rubber sheeting to protect any evidence and placed on a gurney with a blanket over the top to conceal anything that may become visible of the corpse. The scene became very quiet except for the clicking away from Press cameras when the small covered body was brought out of the grove and placed into Truesdale's hearse. Sadness and tears erupted from everyone at the brutal loss of such a charming little girl. The body was transported to the funeral home to await further forensic investigation and autopsy.

The detectives remained at the crime scene to continue to collect anything that could be later found relevant such as the victim's panties, broken tree limbs found at or near the body, and numerous soil samples from under and around the location of the body.

Photographs were taken at every angle not just of the body before its removal (26 photos) but of all the tree branches, footprints and any tire prints from the area.

Unfortunately, forensic science wasn't up to modern standards back in 1955. Much of the crime scene had been contaminated by multiple people moving around the area. It surprised us to see photos of just how many people were allowed to be walking amongst the crime scene.

There weren't footprint castings taken back then; only photos they hoped were relevant. Several areas of the case files state the detectives found the footprints of an adult and a child walking into the pine grove but only adults prints coming back out.

Later on in the investigation, it was admitted that the Prolo children could have possibly disturbed any prints and/or created some of the prints found.

Now comes the hardest part for two different groups of people; the professionals who must autopsy what was left of this once beautiful being and her family, who will now learn their daughter will be coming home, but inside a casket instead running into their loving arms.

The desolate 2-track road leading to the pine grove where Jeannie was discovered.

Photo courtesy of MLive Media Group, and the Kalamazoo Gazette.

Pine Grove where Jeannie was discovered.

Photo courtesy of MLive Media Group, Kalamazoo Gazette, and WMU archives.

Police officers and technicians work to gather evidence at the crime scene.
Photo courtesy of MLive Media Group, Kalamazoo Gazette, and WMU archives.

Jeannie's body being removed from the crime scene.
From the authors' private collection.

FORENSICS – YOUR DECISION

That was a very aesthetic description of the body's condition. We discussed this chapter many times in regards to how we wanted to present it. We are sure detectives informed the Singletons how their precious daughter died, but the question remains as to the extent of details given.

We didn't write this book to glorify horrific and sickening autopsy details for thrill seekers. Knowing surviving family and friends may read this book we were determined to lessen their pain from the forensic details. There are occasions where ignorance is a blessing. We, however, didn't feel we could write a true crime book without discussing the true brutality of the crime.

The decision we came to was to create a separate location for forensics chapter of the book and let the reader decide how much information they would like to read. As stated in the introduction Nicole cried when she first read the autopsy. We would like to spare additional pain to anyone close to Jeannie if possible.

With this in mind if you would like to delve into autopsy details then you can open your internet browser and go to this unpublished link:

OneSilentVoice.com/autopsy.htm

For family and friends who wish to be spared the details, move forward to the next chapter.

CERTIFICATE OF DEATH

MICHIGAN DEPARTMENT OF HEALTH
Vital Records Section

State File No. 107

BIRTH No.

Local File No.

1. PLACE OF DEATH a. COUNTY Allegan	**2. USUAL RESIDENCE** (Where deceased lived. If institution! residence before admission.) a. STATE Michigan b. COUNTY Kalamazoo	
b. CITY (If outside corporate limits, write RURAL and give township) Gunplains — Doster Twp. Twp.	c. LENGTH OF STAY (In this place)	c. TOWNSHIP (Name of) CITY OR VILLAGE Kalamazoo
d. FULL NAME OF HOSPITAL OR INSTITUTION 2 miles N.W. Doster	d. Is Residence within limits of a city or incorporated village? Yes ☒ No ☐	6. STREET ADDRESS 1310 Blakeslee (If rural, give location)
3. NAME OF DECEASED (Type or Print) a. (First) GLORIA b. (Middle) JEAN c. (Last) SINGLETON	**4. DATE OF DEATH** (Month) May (Day) 23, (Year) 1955	
5. SEX female	**6. COLOR OR RACE** white	**7. MARRIED, NEVER MARRIED, WIDOWED, DIVORCED** (Specify) never married	**8. DATE OF BIRTH** Nov. 1, 1946	**9. AGE** (In years last birthday) 8 If under 1 year Months Days If under 24 Hrs. Hours Min.
10a. USUAL OCCUPATION (Give kind of work done during most of working life, even if retired) none	**10b. KIND OF BUSINESS OR INDUSTRY** none	**11. BIRTHPLACE** (State or foreign country) Kalamazoo, Michigan	**12. CITIZEN OF WHAT COUNTRY?** USA
13. FATHER'S NAME Steve Singleton	**14. MOTHER'S MAIDEN NAME** Dorothy Ware	**15. NAME OF HUSBAND OR WIFE OF DECEASED**	
16. WAS DECEASED EVER IN U.S. ARMED FORCES? (Yes, no, or unknown) (If yes, give war or dates of service) no	**17. SOCIAL SECURITY NO.** none	**18. INFORMANT'S NAME** Steve Singleton – Kalamazoo, Michigan	**ADDRESS**

18. CAUSE OF DEATH — MEDICAL CERTIFICATION

Enter only one cause per line for (a), (b), and (c)

I. DISEASE OR CONDITION DIRECTLY LEADING TO DEATH (a) ~~Cause undetermined, pending autopsy report~~ *Manual strangulation*

* This does not mean the mode of dying, such as heart failure, asthenia, etc. It means the disease, injury or complication which caused death.

ANTECEDENT CAUSES Morbid conditions, if any, giving rise to the above cause (a) stating the underlying cause last. DUE TO (b)

DUE TO (c)

II. OTHER SIGNIFICANT CONDITIONS Conditions contributing to the death but not related to the disease or condition causing death.

19a. DATE OF OPERATION	**19b. MAJOR FINDINGS OF OPERATION**	**20. AUTOPSY?** Yes ☒ No ☐

21a. ACCIDENT SUICIDE HOMICIDE (Specify) ~~Rape-Murder~~ Homicide	**21b. PLACE OF INJURY** (e.g., in or about home, farm, factory, street, office bldg., etc.) Farm	**21c. CITY, VILLAGE, OR TOWNSHIP** Gunplains,	**(COUNTY)** Allegan,	**(STATE)** Michigan
21d. TIME OF INJURY (Month) (Day) (Year) 5 – 23 – 55 (Hour)	**21e. INJURY OCCURRED** While at Work ☐ Not While at Work ☐	**21f. HOW DID INJURY OCCUR?** Criminal attack; rape; murder		

22. I hereby certify that I attended the deceased from never , 19 , to , 19 , that I last saw the deceased alive on never , 19 , and that death occurred at m., from the causes and on the date stated above.

23a. SIGNATURE O. A. Dickinson, M. D. (license or title) Med. Examiner – Wayland, Mich.	**23b. ADDRESS**	**23c. DATE SIGNED** June 3, 1955
24a. BURIAL, CREMATION, REMOVAL (Specify) Burial	**24b. DATE** June 3, 1955	**24c. NAME OF CEMETERY OR CREMATORY** Mount Ever-Rest	**24d. LOCATION** (City, village, twp., or county) (State) Kalamazoo, Michigan
DATE REC'D BY LOCAL REG. June 3, 1955	REGISTRAR'S SIGNATURE Esther Hettinger	**25. FUNERAL DIRECTOR'S SIGNATURE**	**ADDRESS**

Dennis F. Langeland – Kalamazoo, Michigan

MARGIN RESERVED FOR BINDING — TYPE OR PRINT (EXCEPT SIGNATURES) IN BLACK INK—THIS IS A PERMANENT RECORD

B-38

**Gloria Jean Singleton's death certificate.
Courtesy of Langland Funeral Home**

OPERATION JEANNIE IS OVER

Parents throughout the state of Michigan woke up on June 2nd, 1955 to hear the news that the body of Jeannie Singleton had been found. Newspapers as far away as Spokane, Washington printed the news that the search and rescue operation had now switched to a homicide investigation

Shock, horror, anger and immense sympathy unknowingly surrounded the Singletons as thousands of people grieved for the family. Family, friends, and neighbors all expressed their sorrow and extended aid in any way possible to get the family through the most difficult time of their lives.

Reports from detectives stated that upon learning the fate of Jeannie the children burst into tears, Dorothy collapsed at the news and needed to be under the care of a physician, and Steve Singleton once again expressed anger towards the perpetrator and told of his desire the killer should be put to death.

A new type of nightmare has now enveloped the Singleton Family; one that no one could alter.

Knowing neither parent could withstand the gut-wrenching reality of seeing their deceased daughter, it was one of Jeannie's uncles who traveled to Truesdale Funeral Home and identified the body. The majority of the planet can only imagine what that experience must have been like and thankfully most of us can live out our days never finding out. The Singleton's weren't given that blessing, especially the brave uncle that volunteered to view little Jeannie.

Despite their immeasurable grief, Jeannie's parents addressed the Kalamazoo Gazette to extend gratitude for all the efforts to find their daughter. The family had received letters and numerous phone calls from distant states giving words of encouragement and continued prayers. The June 2, 1955 newspaper article quoted Dorothy's statement to the public:

> "We are unable to supply words which would adequately express our deepest thanks and appreciation. But we do want the public, all the officers, all the organizations, our neighbors, and every individual to know that we are very grateful. Their sympathy towards our family and their services to us were so comforting and so valuable that we could never repay them. We just want them to know how sincerely grateful we are."

The family would continue to receive comfort from their community while funeral arrangements were made with the help of their church pastor. It was now time to say goodbye.

For the Kalamazoo Police Department, County Sheriff's Office and the Michigan State Police a new truth had to be faced. A child rapist and murderer was stalking their community.

NOW WE LAY HER DOWN TO SLEEP

People gathered graveside to say goodbye to Jeannie.
Photo courtesy of MLive Media Group, and the Kalamazoo Gazette

With the balmy early summer air filled with grief and anguish, the Singletons gathered with family and friends to endure the single worst moment of their lives. Encased in a beautiful flower-draped white casket lay the body of their gentle little girl; a nightmare they never imagined could be possible. Clinging to one another and to their faith, the Singleton family prepared to learn one of God's hardest lessons; how to lead a life without their beloved child, and how to do that without bitterness, anger, and hatred towards God and life itself.

The community of Kalamazoo, with the knowledge that nothing more could be done to bring Jeannie home to her family, banded together to make things as easy as possible for Steve and Dorothy on this dreaded day. The funeral home, now owned by Langeland, gave all services and casket at cost only, the cemetery donated the burial plot, and mountains of flowers were sent by grieving citizens and businesses, including a large floral arrangement sent from Jeannie's class at Woodward School.

Jeannie's pallbearers consisted of the four deacons from the family's New Apostolic Church; Jerry Smith, Thomas Hatfield, Henry Mulder and John Millar. Graciously offering his services to officiate was Bishop Carl Strang from the Chicago New Apostolic Church.

The funeral began at the church on the corner of North Westnedge and Lulu Streets. During this moving service, Reverend Strang recited a passage from the Bible, from the Book of Job, Chapter 1:

> 19 And, behold, there came a great wind from the wilderness and smote the four corners of the house, and it fell upon the young men, and they are dead, and I only am escaped alone to tell thee.
> 21 And Job said, Naked came I out of my mother's womb, and naked shall I return thither: the LORD gave, and the LORD hath taken away; blessed be the name of the LORD.

The clergyman continued to state that he likened that the great wind was that of the spirit of Jeannie's killer. He preached to Jeannie's loved ones that "the law must be left in the hands of the law keepers, and that ours are not to condemn but to consider the source of the sinner's condition."

After the church service was completed and Jeannie loaded into the hearse for her final car ride, the funeral procession began its somber journey four miles south to Mount Ever-Rest Memorial Park. Jeannie's final resting place was a few rows directly in front of a large stone replica of the Bible, a relatively new area in this cemetery and one the owner felt Jeannie deserved – a beautiful place of honor where visitors to the cemetery can be reminded of faith and love.

In a typical Apostolic funeral service the minister would not follow the body to the cemetery but in this tragic case religious etiquette was dismissed, and Reverend Strang wanted to continue his service to the Singleton family at the gravesite. While surrounding the casket at the newly opened earth, he continued his sermon at the gravesite by quoting Thessalonians, Book 1:

> 13 But I would not have you to be ignorant, brethren, concerning them which are asleep, that ye sorrow not, even as others which have no hope.
> 17 Then we which are alive and remain shall be caught up together with them in the clouds, to meet the Lord in the air: and so shall we ever be with the Lord.
> 18 Wherefore comfort one another with these words.

With tears streaming down their faces and tissues drying their eyes, everyone listened as the two hymns, chosen by Dorothy herself, were sung in her daughter's memory – "Beyond the Sunset" and "Follow Me." Lyrics to both hymns can be found in the Appendix.

With solemn words, Reverend Strang concluded the funeral service in stating "the soulless body of the deceased is now surrendered to the Earth."

Quiet prayers and words of sympathy surrounded the Singletons as mourners' tears intermingled with the hugs for the bereaved family; sheer heartbreak clearly seen in the parent's eyes. Eventually, the mourners departed leaving the family in the cemetery; all secretly grateful this was not their own child's memorial service. Throughout Kalamazoo, parents hugged their children a little harder that night.

Whether Jeannie's family was aware or not, several detectives were mingled with mourners at the child's funeral. Not only present to pay their respects, each detective was also silently scanning the attendees and taking notes of whom surrounded the family. Many killers attend the funerals of their victims, and they hoped perhaps Jeannie's would do the same.

As for Steve and Dorothy, they now faced the second hardest thing a parent has to endure; leaving their young child's body buried in the ground. As a mother, the feeling you are abandoning your child to the coldest darkness imaginable can be just as heart-wrenching as the final goodbye. Eventually, the Singletons, with their arms around the children and trying to remain strong, turned and walked out of the cemetery, leaving their beloved Jeannie behind for the last time.

The Singleton family grieves for Jeannie surrounded by friends.
Photo courtesy of MLive Media Group, and the Kalamazoo Gazette.

A GENTLE ROSE

What bell does toll the passing of a child?
A life so young so pure...unreconciled
That death should grasp her now without remorse
Just as her life sets sail its rocky course
Come Terpsichore and sing your songs of dance
And curse the evil Thanatos whose lance
Strikes deep into the mourners grieving soul
Rise up I pray, her life I do extol
A gentle rose whose beauty graced this earth
A loving soul, so caring full of mirth
I beg of thee, no songs of sorrow weep
But shout our hymns of praise, so all might keep
Her in our hearts for e'er, for we have known
A gentle rose, that God now calls his own

-Tim Chambers; used with permission

SO MANY QUESTIONS:
SO FEW ANSWERS

We found it truly amazing the number of potential witnesses that came out of the woodwork after Jeannie's body was found. Perhaps knowing she was murdered instead of just a young girl missing sparked some memories hidden within their day-to-day lives.

Numerous statements came pouring in about two suspicious cars that were in the Blakeslee/ Douglas Street neighborhoods on the day of Jeannie's disappearance – a blue Chevy and a yellow car. The witness accounts of a blue Chevy being driven by a sandy-hair gentleman, sometimes wearing a pair of glasses or sunglasses, began to build at an alarming rate.

Police re-interviewed a substantial amount of known and rumored sex offenders and homosexuals about their alibis. Person after person were escorted in to take lie detectors tests. While a few of these interrogation results in some violations none of them seemed to pertain to the Singleton case.

On June 7th, a call came in about a suspicious man trying to give young girls a "ride home." Officer Lanphear responded and spoke with two teenage girls who reported that they were drawn to a 1952 blue Chevy sitting on Frank Street, just east of Burdick. They described the young man as having brownish hair and wearing a grey work shirt. The two girls watched as the man in question stopped numerous white and black girls, ranging in age from 6 – 10 years of age, telling them to get into his car for a ride home. Thankfully none of the little girls took him up on his offer, but the gentleman kept up this game long enough for the two teenagers bystanders to not only get a good look at the man but was able to remember his license plate of NC 61-73.

Officer Lanphear radioed in this information, and only a half hour later he was informed the suspicious vehicle was pulled over by Officers Joyce and Thompson and placed the man under arrest. Officer Joyce escorted the suspect in the squad vehicle while Thompson drove the suspect's car to the Kalamazoo Police Department.

Lanphear brought both teenage girls into the station for identification of the man they saw earlier. Both girls not only positively identified the blue car but also identified the man. This man was Eugene Ray O'Connell, a prison parolee.

Transcripts of Eugene O'Connell's interrogation were not present in the Singleton case files, only witness statements and his arrest record were provided. It is known the suspect was given and passed a lie detector test in regards to Jeannie, but a final investigation memo on June 20th stated the fate of Mr. O'Connell after interrogations ended. He was officially arrested for accosting females and was returned to prison as a parole violator. It doesn't look like the teenagers helped to find Jeannie's killer, but they did succeed in taking a stalking pedophile off the streets before he could harm anyone else.

Two days later a Michigan State Police Detective called the Kalamazoo PD about an arrest they made in Otsego. Bernard Mollitor was apprehended and charged with attempted rape of his five-year-old daughter.

Officer Cleveland took down the report and brought Mr. Mollitor in for questioning. This suspect was on parole from a previous conviction that landed him in Jackson prison for 2-15 years. A lie detector test administered at the State Police Post in Paw Paw proved this child rapist and nothing to do with Jeannie's demise, but this man was clearly returning back to Jackson for his previous charge.

The Kalamazoo Sheriff's Department was the next facility to receive a promising lead. An Indian who goes by the name of Chuch was drinking heavily at Hooper Bear Tavern and began making several remarks of a young girl lying under some pine trees. Several more sober patrons remembered his remarks and called the sheriff's office the next morning.

Chuch, legally known as Charles Wabanimkee, was a 33 year- old married man and father of two children. Born and raised on Beaver Island he was unable to make a good living on the island, so he eventually moved to Charlevoix at the age of 17. Immediately following his departure to the mainland, he was drafted into the Armed Forces and transferred to England where he met his wife, Joan. After being discharged in November 1945, Chuch settled with his future wife in Grand Rapids, Michigan.

The couple eventually married and became parents of a boy and a girl. However, all was not blissful in the Wabanimkee home as Chuch's habit of drinking with the guys turned into full-blown alcoholism mixed with a tendency to not come home for a day or two. His marriage was failing fast.

It was during a two-day drinking binge with some people he met at a buddy's house in Ada that led to his drunken remarks in a tavern 25 miles away. Starting at his friend's Hawley's house, he traveled to another establishment where he met a woman and her friend Wally. The three new friends, after hours of drinking, decided to travel to Lakeview where more drinking took place.

After leaving this bar, the trio was driving on back roads when Wally lost vision of the road on this foggy night and ran off the road hitting a couple of bushes causing some damage to the passenger door. When the car came to a halt, instead of getting out of the car, they decided to stay put and sleep the rest of the night away under tall pine trees.

Upon waking the next morning, they traveled back to Hawley's house where Wabanimkee got back into his car and returned home. Feeling very sick from his two-day binge he called in sick with his employer but was awakened hours later by his irate wife and two police officers who dragged him to Kalamazoo for questioning.

Wabanimkee was held for 24 hours for questioning and a lie detector test. He passed both with flying colors, and the detectives were convinced his remarks had nothing to do with Jeannie's case; just a bunch of drunken rambling and he was brought back to his home in Grand Rapids to face the wrath of his wife.

Drink binges and the inevitable incoherent ramblings they cause became a problem for the officials' investigating the murder case. Officers soon found themselves traveling all over Michigan when a police department called them about a possible lead. Some of these trips took them to Detroit and sometimes across the state lines into

Indiana. Each one of these visit not only entailed hours of investigation and fact checking but also locating someplace for each suspect to be administered the lie detector test. Grueling hours of travel piled up with no results and the detectives grew more frustrated as the days went on.

In 1955 it seems, just having marital problems stemming from a bad sexual relationship with your spouse, but preferring instead to be aroused by pornography, was enough suspicion to have you hauled in for questioning.

A report came in of a suspicious man in a 1950 Chevrolet driving slowly around the Sunshine Gardens Nudist Camp. When police arrived, they did indeed spot the lurking car and pulled the driver over for questioning. The driver, Conrad Hutzell, claimed he had visited the Nudist Camp the year before and was checking on a rumor that the camp was no longer in operation. Writing down his personal information, and noting the car actually belonged to Mrs. Hutzell, they allowed him to continue on his way.

The following day they contacted Mrs. Hutzell who obviously wasn't shy about discussing the reasons why her marriage failed, and in fact, the couple had just become divorced. She allowed her ex-husband who didn't own a car of his own to borrow hers when looking for a job.

The former wife informed the officers that her husband was mentally unbalanced and possibly homosexual. Whenever her husband would go into the bathroom and take a bath, he would take his collection of nude photos of women in with him. She readily admitted that for the past year she could not stand her husband to touch her and left him to his own ways of taking care of his needs.

Traveling back to Mr. Hutzell's apartment on South Rose Street he validated everything his former spouse said including the fact he had been having a relationship with a man in Toledo. When police checked this man's criminal record, they found absolutely nothing; not even a parking ticket. Coupled with the information of his new sexual preference plus the fact he did not own a car nor borrow the ex-wife's car on May 23rd, he was cleared of all suspicion with the murder investigation immediately.

In some cases witnessed innocent actions can also be construed as suspicious by others. No one learned that lesson better than Lawrence Booth. Mr. Booth's mother-in-law noticed her daughter's husband painting his car from a dark brown to black the day following Jeannie Singleton's disappearance. Booth held a previous criminal charge from 1949 of larceny and was probably not highly welcomed into the wife's family. This disgruntled relative also informed police that Booth lived on Church St in Kalamazoo. Police jumped right on this statement and began to hunt down Lawrence Booth with a vengeance, only to find the man did not live in Kalamazoo but in Grand Rapids and his motive for painting his car was nothing more than a desire to make repairs and have a different colored car. His employer in Grand Rapids further proved that Booth had worked a 10 ½ hour shift on May 23rd. Makes you wonder what else this vindictive mother-in-law did back then to thwart her daughter's marriage to him!

We learned quickly while perusing the crime file that it didn't take much to get under a detective's radar. As mentioned earlier if you were homosexual you were on the radar automatically. If you ever committed a crime, you were on the radar. If you decided to skip work on May 23rd, 1955, you went on the radar. If you talked about the case in public in such a way to make it sound as if you knew something, citizens put you on the radar. If you decided to drive out to Doster to see the infamous site where Jeannie was discovered you really put yourself on the radar! Such minor suspects continued to cross paths with authorities in regards to this case because of small insignificant reasons. They are so numerous in numbers in the Singleton case file that we decided to only mention the most significant suspects.

In February 1956 Leonard Fults slipped onto the radar when several reports came in with regards to the man's desire to expose his genitals. Married with three children, Fults and his wife worked as attendants at the Kalamazoo State Hospital. This man did have prior criminal offenses for DUIs and reckless driving, but nothing close to violent convictions.

Upon detention of Mr. Fults, he was questioned and given a lie detector test. While the polygraph gave no indication he knew anything regarding Jeannie, it did bring out his sexual desire for exposure. He admitted that he loved walking around the house nude when his wife and children were out of the house. While naked he would open the curtains in front of the large window at the 804 Gilbert house and allowed any passersby to catch a glimpse of his genitalia. Fults admitted to having affairs with other women, but his ultimate fantasy was to have a sexual encounter with a stranger who witnessed him in the window. His sexual cravings didn't catch a willing stranger, but it did catch a criminal conviction of indecent exposure.

Found within the case file was one page of correspondence from the City of Roanoke, Virginia about one Frank J. Snider. It was obvious from this letter that prior correspondences between the two police departments took place, but these letters were not included in the case file. The only correlation we could find was a small mention of Snider having a brother who resided in Michigan.

This lone memo stated that Snider was found guilty on June 25, 1955, of savagely raping a 9-year-old girl and the jury fixed his punishment as death in the electric chair due to the child's excessive injuries and trauma. His expected date of execution was set for August 3, 1956, at the Virginia State Penitentiary in Richmond.

Due to numerous appeals, the execution of Frank Snider did not occur in 1956. I located a 1967 denial of appeal which stated Snider was attempting to be transferred out of prison and into a state psychiatric hospital feigning insanity as his reasoning for the rape. Four psychiatrists determined that Snider had "a sociopathic personality, but without any psychosis."

A 1982 Washington Post article on Snider's case told how the convicted former steelworker "ate his last meal" three separate times, but his life was spared within hours of the electric chair. His wife had promptly divorced him after his conviction and hasn't seen his children since. Frank Jimmy Snider died of a heart attack in August 1986 at the age of 59.

37-year-old David Dunlap was already incarcerated in the Hastings County Jail when he fell onto Kalamazoo's radar.

In August 1958, Dunlap was picked up by Hasting's Sheriff Department when a 16-year-old reported that while walking down the road, a mile and a half east of Doster, Dunlap offered her a ride. The teenager refused, but Dunlap wasn't finished with his propositions. Following her, Dunlap showed her a condom and asked if she knew what it was. When then girl stated she didn't know what the item was, Dunlap offered to show her how to use one. When the young girl said no again, Dunlap got out of his car. Thinking quickly, the teenage girl told him that her mother was working in a nearby field picking berries, and proceeded to run into the field calling out for her mother. After a small chase by Dunlap, the man eventually gave up and drove away.

This incident came to the Kalamazoo police attention not only because of the nature of the offense, which Dunlap denied, but because the location was near where Jeannie's body was discovered. After learning Dunlap had taken the week of May 23rd, 1955 off work at Valley Metal Products in Plainwell, Detective Dykehouse decided to pay the gentleman a visit.

Upon questioning Dunlap about the week of May 23rd, he denied any connection to the Jeannie Singleton murder, and in fact, he recalled that he and his family paid a visit to relatives in Kentucky during that time. Even though this alibi would put the suspect out of the state at the time of Jeannie's murder, the mention of a trip could never be definitely substantiated. Dunlap did, however, remark that he was aware of where Jeannie's body had been located, as he and his wife would often park in that area before they were married. Upon request, Dunlap agreed to take a polygraph test.

On August 27th, Dunlap was transported to Rockford where he was administered a polygraph examination by Detective Menzies. The first chart showed deception when questioned about the Hastings case and the Singleton case. A more in-depth interrogation commenced where Dunlap once again denied any sexual perversion. Eventually, after failing yet another polygraph examination, Dunlap realized if he continued to deny any allegations or suspicions, he would be regarded as a major suspect in the Singleton case.

After repeated urgings from Detective Dykehouse, Dunlap admitted to the Hastings case, claiming that everything the young teenager had stated in the report was true and his full intent was to rape the 16-year old that day. Dunlap also admitted trying to pick up younger girls in the Yankee Springs area, but when he exposed himself to them, they had become frightened and ran away.

Once Dunlap had relieved himself of all guilt from his indecent transgressions, a polygraph examination was again administered. This time the test showed no deceptions, and Detective Menzies stated he felt there was no connection to the Singleton case. Before departing Rockford, Detective Dykehouse notified Hastings Prosecuting Attorney that Dunlap admitted to the charges in Hastings. David Dunlop was ultimately convicted and sentenced to four years in prison.

In October 1961, Kalamazoo detectives received a call from a woman who refused to identify herself. She stated she had information which led her to believe a gentleman named Glen Lucas could be guilty of the Singleton murder. When attempting to gain more information from her, she simply stated that she didn't wish to become involved and hung up.

The next day this same woman called again to find out if the police were looking into Lucas. When the call was transferred to Detective Dykehouse, he finally convinced her to meet with him at the bureau later that day.

The mystery woman, whose name was Beverly, arrived as promised. She told detectives that she is the former step-daughter of Glen Lucas. While living on Frances Street in late 1938, she testified that Lucas had raped her and then two years later, at the age of eleven, had raped her again. Lucas informed her on both occasions if Beverly ever told anyone he would beat her and her sister, RuthAnn. Frightened for her sister and mother's safety, she told no one about the abuse she had suffered.

Years later, when the two girls grew into teenagers, Beverly opened up to her older sister and was shocked to discover that RuthAnn had been raped as well by Lucas when she was younger. Neither girl had told their secret to anyone, not even their mother. Sadly, there was a third daughter in the picture, even younger than Beverly.

Lucas soon divorced the girl's mother, Thelma, and entered into two other marriages. One with a woman named Mildred and finally to his then-current wife, Nancy. Nancy and Glen would often come to Thelma's home to pick up the youngest daughter, Darlene, for visitation; overnight visitations.

In September 1961, Thelma was surprised when Nancy visited the home without Glen and informed her she had left her husband two weeks prior. Then to Thelma's astonishment, Nancy warned her about allowing Glen to see his daughter alone as 9 month's prior Glen had told Nancy in a drunken state that he had killed Jeannie Singleton and threatened to kill his wife if she told anyone. Nevertheless, Nancy felt Thelma deserved a warning should anything happen to Darlene.

Later that evening, Thelma broke down and told Beverly what Nancy had told her. Knowing what Glen had done to her and his sister in the past; Beverly had no problems believing Lucas could have killed Jeannie and therefore called the police the next day.

Detective Dykehouse paid a visit to Nancy Lucas, and she verified Beverly's story stating that she had married Lucas in 1956 and that before marrying him, had been employed at Fairmont Tuberculosis Hospital; one the hospitals used to teach the nursing classes Dorothy Singleton was attending at the time of Jeannie's death. She was aware of who Mrs. Singleton was even before her daughter was murdered.

After the marriage of Glen Lucas and Nancy, Lucas drank considerably and would often get up in the middle of the night to drink some more. In the early months of 1956, Nancy confronted this husband-turned-stranger and asked why he was always drinking; what was the issue? His reply back to her was, "he had something on his mind and that this was why he was always drinking, but maybe he would feel better if he told her about it." He proceed to inform his startled wife that he had killed little Jeannie Singleton and if Nancy told anyone what he said that he would "kill her too."

Nancy couldn't believe what she was being told and when she asked her husband why he had killed the girl, she was more shocked when Glen told her it was "her fault." Sitting in disbelief, Nancy informed Glen that in May 1955 they had not been dating yet so how was it her fault? Glen continued on with a completely irrational story of how he knew who Nancy was from a mutual friend and would often drive through the Douglas neighborhood to watch Nancy walk to work. He was becoming frustrated with his inability to just knock on Nancy's door, introduce himself and asked her out on a date. This frustration grew until one day while driving around the neighborhood waiting for Nancy to appear, he spotted the "crippled little girl on Blakeslee and picked her up."

By this time Nancy was not only beginning to believe in her husband's story but coming to the realization of just what her husband may be capable of. When she asked him further why he felt the need to kill her, Lucas stated that the little girl "Got smart and started lipping off to him," so he had killed her. He continued to boast that he had taken his wife driving by the spot he killed the girl many times.

The next morning, Beverly and Nancy accompanied Det. Dykehouse in his car and went for a ride through the countryside. He told Nancy that although there was a certain area he wanted to drive by he would not take her there immediately, nor would it be the last location they went by. If an area seemed familiar to Nancy as a place Lucas would take her for rides, he wanted to be informed. The leisurely ride with the Detective took over three hours as they drove all over northern Kalamazoo County and southern Allegan County.

While driving down Marsh Rd, in the direction of Pine Lake, Nancy stated that this territory looked familiar to her, that she and Lucas had often driven through here. She became more adamant when they reached the dirt road leading to Doster. Once in Doster, they turned on one of the main dirt roads. The one that had the "little wagon tracks" that lead to where Jeannie was found. Nancy told Detective Dykehouse that she had been there with her husband. When the Detective pulled off to a spot in the pines, Nancy said she had been there with Lucas, and he had called it "Lover's Land." Nancy had volunteered all this information to the Detective without the officer making a single suggestion.

I can only imagine the thoughts that must have been swirling around Detective Dykehouse's mind during the continued ride through the Plainwell countryside and back to the police station. "Lover's Land" was the only mere feet away from where Jeannie's body was discovered!

Back at the station, the officer interviewed RuthAnn who confirmed everything Beverly had told him. Lucas had forced intercourse on her since she was 7 years old until she was sixteen. When RuthAnn was a small child she had even contracted gonorrhea from Lucas; a fact also confirmed by Beverly.

All of these strong women told police they would be willing to confront Lucas about what he had done to them and perhaps catch him in a statement about the Singleton case. It was decided by the Captain they would use Nancy in an attempt to get information from Lucas.

The police secured two apartments, 200 & 203, at 259 Portage Street. Room 203 was wired for sound and the receiver placed in Room 200; Nancy was to pretend she had been living in Room 203 ever since leaving Lucas.

Beverly was set up to "casually" run into Lucas and nonchalantly tell him she had recently run into Nancy and that she had been staying in Room 203 at the Portage Street address.

Lucas took the bait, and a couple of night later he was waiting for Nancy outside of her new apartment on Portage Street. Nancy and Lucas went inside and talked until approximately 9:00pm when he left. Nancy had occasionally tried to get her husband to talk about the Singleton case, but Lucas stated several times he had no clue as to what she was talking about. The stake-out was a bust.

Next, the detectives decided to gain more psychological information from Nancy about her husband's sexual tendencies. She admitted that her husband's sex drive was not that strong, but when they did engage in sex, he would become violent and beat her or viciously bite her. On two occasions Lucas had taken a knife and cut her during sex.

After this astounding confession, Nancy mentioned they had a 14-year-old neighbor, Virginia Libbey while living on Oak Street. Nancy had become suspicious that something immoral may have been going on as her husband seemed to pay extra attention to this teenager. An interview with Virginia's mother claimed Lucas would take his daughter Darlene and her daughter swimming from time to time. However, her daughter had never mentioned anything inappropriate. She strenuously claimed that her daughter would never do anything out of line. Strangely, there is nothing in the Singleton case file that references detective ever talked with Virginia.

After the police had questioned every female associated with Lucas and found that no one had a good thing to say about the man, it was time to bring the suspect in. Lucas was arrested on November 8th at his mother's house on North Church St and brought in to the Kalamazoo Police Station. At the station, he denied having anything to do with the

Singleton girl He also denied molesting anyone or having intercourse with his step-children. He further denied telling Nancy he was Jeannie's killer. Lucas went as far as to deny that he drank at all and agreed to take a polygraph test to prove it.

When the lie detector showed signs of deception when asked about the Singleton case, Lucas was formally booked and held on charges of investigation of murder.

The following day Lucas again denied every accusation that was ever mentioned, but the police went one step further and brought in every woman he had ever wronged. Beverly was escorted into the room where she screamed about him raping her when she was a small child. To her face, he insisted none of it was true.

RuthAnn was then escorted into the interrogation room where she accused him of having intercourse with her from the age of 7 until she was 16. Despite tearfully shouting out details of every violation done to her, Lucas denied every aspect of it.

Finally his wife Nancy was led into the room where she coldly accused him of telling her how he killed Jeannie Singleton; he denied this. When she cried and yelled about all the times he had beaten her during sex he refused to admit to a single thing.

Having witnessed the raw emotion from all three women, there were no doubt in the detectives' minds the ladies were telling the truth. After hours of intense questioning by the police, Lucas finally admitted to drinking heavily and to only a few indiscretions with RuthAnn but would admit to nothing further.

The coming days produced no further evidence. To the discouragement of detectives; Glen Lucas, a sexual monster, was released from custody.

Decades flew by, and only a sparse number of suspects came to light. One serious suspect appeared in 1973; a suspect so foul that it will be easy to conclude that he must be Jeannie's murderer.

DECADES OF SILENCE

The Singleton case suddenly became the main focus in Detective Frank Whitaker's mind when in 1973, a woman came forward with the claim her deceased husband, a former part-time Allegan County Army recruiter, was probably the murderer of little Jeannie. Many of the incidents listed below stem from Velma Fox's statements and her polygraph test results in 1973.

Velma Fox was the main target of her husband's Georges anger. She was the victim of physical and emotional abuse throughout their marriage. Velma, however, wasn't George's only victim. He would on several occasions take pleasure taking his sexual aggressions out on very young females. Three of these young victims were his daughters, all of whom died before the age of six months. His wife reports having caught him molesting his older children several times, each time he had promised the children candy in exchange for their silence.

We were able to find the death records for all four of the infants who died of seemingly normal conditions:

- 1920 – Elizabeth, 7 days old. Died of "bowel infection from an unknown source."

- 1921 – Julia, 2 months old. Died of indigestion.

- 1929 – Mildred, 23 days old. Died of bronchitis.

- 1931 – Francis, 5 months old. Died of "internal injuries."

Velma herself was a victim of George's unnatural libido and sadist tendencies; she was forced to give her husband sex twice a day, every day. She was also often sexually assaulted by her husband. According to Velma, there was an incident during which her husband shoved a flashlight inside her, in an attempt to see what women's "insides" look like. It is sad to think of the terror this woman was subjected to on a daily basis.

Both of George's brothers also had arrest records for sex crimes. This leads us to conclude that it is very likely this was a family trait, perhaps even a genetic predisposition for sexual deviancy. Here is an abbreviated list of crimes that demonstrate just how big of a monster George truly was:

- George was charged with a 1937 rape where the victim was also badly beaten.

- In 1948, while living in Allegan County, Velma's teenage sister Laverna was assaulted by George. He tried to rape Laverna after striking her with his fist and knocking her onto a bed. This atrocity was witnessed by one of the Fox children who immediately reported the incident to their mother. Velma soon sent her sister away from the home to keep her safe. The incident however surprisingly went unreported to authorities.

- In 1953, while the Fox family was in Orlando Florida, George had a forced sexual relationship with a 20-year old woman. This assault resulted in pregnancy. Luckily for the baby, the Fox family returned to Michigan. This baby wouldn't be another victim of their sadistic father.

Two years later it would be 1955; a time when according to Velma George may have been involved in the murder of Jeannie. In May 1955, George was working part-time in the Kalamazoo area. His daily commute put George on Douglas Avenue around the same time Jeannie and the other neighborhood children would be walking home from school. Not only was he in the area on a daily basis but according to Velma, George would become excited, each time he heard a news story about Jeannie's disappearance. That excitement grew each day as more reports were discussed in the news. Velma also mentioned that George took her on a small road trip up Blakeslee Street so he could show her the house where Jeannie lived.

Velma told Detective Whitaker that on June 1st, 1955, George had become very animated and ordered her in the car for yet another short road trip. This time the trip which occurred around at dusk, ended in the small town of Doster. Velma noticed there were multiple police cars, unmarked vehicles and a hearse parked on a small street. The hearse according to Velma was backed up on a little path with the back of the car positioned near the pine trees.

During her interrogation on June 15, 1973, Capt. R. Stewart talked with Velma. He confirmed that she had described the exact spot where Jeannie's body was located, as well as the position of the vehicles at the scene that evening. As the questioning continued, Velma told Detective Whitaker that in addition to George mysteriously knowing right where Jeannie's body was located, he also stated very matter-of-factly to Velma that the young girl had been sexually assaulted. This statement intrigued the detective. If it were true how had George known about the rape? Jeannie's sexual assault was not public knowledge. How could George have known such detail even before the medical examiner had a chance to perform his duties?

George's growing macabre obsession with Jennie did not go unnoticed by Velma, and her suspicion of George's possible involvement in the Singleton murder increased. In early 1959, after Velma reports she had received a particularly harsh beating, Mrs. Fox accused her husband of killing the girl. George's reply according to Velma was "Keep your mouth shut, or I will get you." Later that year in August, once again following a brutal physical assault, Velma again challenged her husband. This time she told him "You are oversexed and killed the little girl, I am just glad that someday you will get caught."

According to Velma's statement, George's reply to his wife's accusations was "They will never solve it." In neither case according to Velma had she ever mentioned Jeannie by name; George just automatically knew who she was talking about.

By the end of 1959, George had grown tired of his wife's constant accusations and decided to teach her a lesson she would not forget.

On New Year's Eve, George drove Velma out to the area where Jeannie's body had been found, and viciously raped his wife, ending it with a brutal anal attack.

As she had in the past after being victimized by her husband, Velma was silent and didn't tell a soul about the New Year's Eve incident. With as many beatings as Velma described during her marriage, it is likely that fresh bruises were no longer a surprise to family members or friends. This time, however, would be different. Velma suffered internal injuries that couldn't be ignored. Six days after the sadistic attack by her husband, while they were in Texas away from local friends, Velma took herself to the Lakeview Hospital's Emergency Room in Augusta, Texas for treatment.

Detective Whitaker assigned a Kalamazoo pathologist to request the medical records from Augusta, Texas and review them to help to either confirm or disprove Velma's testimony. The report that was received by the detective told a tale of unspeakable pain and humiliation, an assault beyond the description offered to him by Velma.

According to the medical report from January 6, 1959, Velma Fox was admitted for severe bleeding from her genitals. The medical report documented open sores on her uterus, acute tenderness of the stomach, and extreme tearing of the vaginal and anal walls. All of those injuries substantiate a forcible vaginal and anal rape, which proved to Detective Whitaker that the incident on New Year's Eve did indeed occur.

The Texas physician also personally noted that it appeared Velma was "ripped apart from the inside out," an object like a large stick or branch was used in the rape. Splinters from this branch being inserted inside the woman's vagina were found lodged in the soft tissue and had caused a massive infection.

We have to assume that Detective Whitaker found the use of the branch to be an important clue, just as we did since broken tree branches were noted on the list of evidence collected at Jeannie's murder site. Furthermore, it was stated in the final autopsy reports that based on the position of Jeannie's body, anal rape was likely the last deed committed on her poor little body before her death.

The polygraph test administered to Velma on July 26, 1973, confirmed what detectives already suspected, she was telling the truth. What also amazed the detectives was the fact that the tests also showed despite all the horrific abuse suffered throughout the years, and the guilt and grief associated with their deceased babies, Velma still fiercely loved her husband. Loved him so much in fact that she waited nine years after George's death of cancer in 1962 before coming forward with her suspicions.

It is hard for anyone who has never been the victim of relationship abuse to understand why Velma had not come forward in 1955, or at any time during the next 18 years she was with George. According to experts, there are many possible reasons. Among them:

- She may have had a false sense that telling on him would mean she didn't love him.

- She might have feared he would kill her if she spoke.

- She may have feared he would harm the remaining children.

- She also may have after years of abuse just gotten so used to violence that even the murder seemed to be just another part of being married.

When we first read through the case files, we were convinced that George Fox was the last person Jeannie had ever seen. We do have to admit that to us the facts sure make him look guilty. There were, however, others that were equally as good a fit. In fact, we were even approached by the family of another

Kalamazoo man in 2014. They wanted to know if it looked as if the murder could have been done by one of their deceased relatives, Fred Davis. After hearing about Fred, it was clear to us that this man was just as much a monster as George Fox. We would soon however hear from two separate officers one who worked the case in 1955 and one who is currently assigned the case as part of Michigan State Police Cold Case Team, that there is no doubt in either of their minds who killed Jeannie, and it isn't anyone we have discussed in detail up to this point.

ONE SUSPECT EMERGES

In the early afternoon of May 23, 1955, 14-year-old Malinda Miller and her two younger brothers ate a quick lunch and left to return to Woodward school. It was at this time that a man in a blue car whistled at her three times. Malinda remembered this strange encounter happened near the corner of Douglas and Ravine Rd. Ignoring the man the children continued walking south on Douglas Ave. When the children arrive on the sidewalk in front of an Adult Foster Care house, the same man slowed his vehicle down and proceeded to whistle at Malinda again.

By this time Malinda was becoming a little unnerved with the stranger and the children walked faster towards school. At the corner of Blakeslee and Douglas, Malinda met up with one of her girlfriends, when all five children noticed the same blue car parked on the southwest corner. The man was sitting behind the wheel staring at the children. His gaze seemed to be fixed on Malinda.

Later that same day at approximately 3:45pm Malinda, her two brothers, and friend Linda Vandenburg began walking north on Douglas. It was at this time that she observed the same car from earlier in the day. The car pulled up alongside the girls, and the occupant motioned for Malinda to get in the car, and he would give her a ride. Malinda, however, was smart enough to know better and declined his invitation. When he demanded to know "What's the matter with you?" she promptly answered, "I only have one block left to walk." The man then mumbled incoherently, laughed angrily and drove away quickly. This gentleman's advances were witnessed by many people including Ronald Roeder who just so happened to be Detective Gerlof's nephew.

What Malinda and her brothers couldn't have known was this same man had been cruising around Lincoln School earlier, around 3:20pm, on that same afternoon. The stranger slid his car next to where Mary Meyers was preparing to cross the road and asked the young girl to come to the car. As she approached the vehicle, the man stated: "Your mother and father asked me to pick you up from school."

This statement drew instant red flags with Mary, especially since she only lived with her mother and didn't have a father at home. She told the man "My parents would never ask anyone to give me a ride home, I live right across the street from the school. " Angrily the man sped off.

Despite the close call, Mary had with her potential abductor her closeness to the man would be instrumental in giving the police the best description. The driver was described as a white male, 24 to 35 years of age, short reddish-sandy colored hair, light complexion with a long thin face, possibly wearing glasses/ sunglasses, well built and dressed in a light grey shirt and grey pair of pants. The car in question was a dark blue 1953 or 1954 Chevrolet with a small radio antenna on the left side of the car, just forward of the door. She also stated that the car had a faulty muffler. Detective Gerlof's nephew gave a further description of the car as being a Chevy Tudor with completely black tires.

The hunt for this unidentified man was underway. With the help of eyewitness accounts, two sketches of this mysterious individual were featured in the Kalamazoo Gazette. One sketch showed the gentleman wearing glasses while the other wearing sunglasses. These sketches ended up becoming more valuable than anyone could have known.

The day after little Jeannie's body was discovered, while the Singleton Family was still reeling in grief and shock, Reverend Victor Gold ventured into the Kalamazoo Police Station to discuss one of his parishioners.

Captain Stewart sat down with the clergyman and learned one of the church parishioners had come to him for advice. He had admitted to the minister that he was the man who had accosted Malinda Miller. Mr. Stanley Edgerton would be coming in soon, with his minister in tow, to confess to being the gentleman they were seeking. Interestingly enough Edgerton did not arrive at the station until Jun 9th.

Stan Edgerton was a 29-year-old married father of two children who had worked for the Upjohn Corporation for years. His current residence was 1409 Hamelink Drive, Kalamazoo and he owned a 1953 dark blue Chevrolet, the exact car described in the newspaper.

Detective Dykehouse informed Edgerton they wanted to have a written statement on file. All questions and any answers given were being recorded in shorthand by a stenographer after which would be transcribed and typewritten so the suspect could read the statement and sign. Edgerton agreed with this method, and the questioning began. Below is the true word-for-word account of that interrogation which Stanley Edgerton read and signed.

Q. Your name is Stanley Edgerton?
A. Yes, sir.
Q. And you live where?
A. 1409 Hamelink
Q. And you are employed at the Upjohn Company?
A. Yes Sir. On Henrietta St., Dept. 81-1
Q. Are you married?
A. Yes
Q. What is your wife's name?
A. Jeanne
Q. How old is your wife?
A. 30
Q. Any children?
A. Yes, Steven age 3 ½ and Deborah, age 1 ½
Q. How long have you been employed with UpJohn?
A. Four years
Q. No threats or promises have been made to you in regards to questioning?
A. No sir.
Q. This is being done of your own free will?
A. Yes.
Q. The day we are talking about is Monday, May 23. Is that correct?
A. I assume that it was. It may have been.
Q. Do you recall whether it was the day the Singleton girl disappeared?
A. No.
Q. Do you remember whether it was the day before you read about the Singleton girl's disappearance in the paper?
A. No.
Q. But you do know it was about that time?
A. Yes.
Q. Do you know if it was the same week?
A. I think I can say yes on that.
Q. Do you know if it was Monday or Tuesday?

A. No sir. I know it was a day or so from the time Jeannie Singleton disappeared – one way or the other. I know it wasn't Saturday or Sunday. I read that you were looking for a man who had attempted to pick up some girls in that area and after seeing the sketch and description of the man and car involved, knew I was that person.

Q. What kind of car have you got?

A. 53 Chevy, dark blue

Q. Can you tell us what you were doing on this date in question to make you think you were the man referring to?

A. Assuming it was Monday, I spent a normal working Monday.

Q. What hours do you work?

A. 8:00am to 5:00pm.

Q. What did you do on this day which you are assuming was Monday?

A. At noon I had lunch at the plant cafeteria as usual. Afterward took my car, drove across town to deliver some repaired equipment to the Newman Visual Education Co. on 783 W. Main Street, and then intended to go to the Electrical Supply Corporation located at 906 E. Michigan. I left the equipment and then decided to take a drive. I drove out to Douglas, and somewhere on Douglas Avenue between North St and Alamo Ave. I observed a teenager walking along and glancing at said teenager, smiled. She smiled. I whistled and drove on – not too far. Turned around the block and came back again, smiled, whistled and followed her up the street.

Q. Did you open the car door and ask her to get in?

A. I know I didn't open the door. I assume the windows were down. I don't recall whether I asked her to get in the car or not. I took a couple of more turns around the area the girl was in and drove on north then back to town.

Q. How many times did you whistle and talk to her?

A. Two or three times. I returned to the UpJohn plant where I work, went back to work about 1:00pm and worked until approximately 3:00pm, then decided to take a breaking time to go to the Electrical Supply as I had forgotten to do so on my noon trip. Then I got in the wrong lane of traffic and missed my turn on a one-way street and forced through the center of town. Having come through the center of town and being quite disgusted with the traffic situation, I said to myself: "To heck with it," and drove around with no particular destination in view. Subconsciously I found myself back in the Woodward School area and driving out Douglas. I again probably went as far as Ravine Rd, turned around, and headed back toward town again, unintentionally encountering the same girl I had seen at noon, smiled and whistled. The out of the clear blue it hit me that it was pretty ridiculous, got cold feet and got out of the area.

Q. What did you say to the girl on the second encounter?

A. I don't know.

Q. Did you stop the car?

A. I don't think so. I may have been going at walking speed.

Q. You say you realized the ridiculous situation you were getting yourself into. Can you explain that? What was ridiculous about it?

A. I just realized I was a married man trying to pick up a girl.

Q. You don't recall what you said to the girl?

A. No.

Q. Do you recall what your intentions were?

A. Well, I know that my intentions were anything but honorable.

Q. Did you intend to pick the girl up if possible?

A. My intentions before meeting the girl in the afternoon would have been to pick her up. Upon seeing her in the afternoon, I realized what a ridiculous situation I was getting myself involved in and got out of the area, returning to the plant.

Q. But you must have at least implied or gotten your thoughts across to the girl that you intended to pick up.

A. I was driving slow and probably said: "Do you want a ride? How about a ride?" or a like remark.

Q. What time did you arrive at the plant?

A. I probably arrived at the plant no later than 4:00pm.

Q. Was there anyone at the plant who can verify your coming in there around 4 o'clock?

A. I don't think so, sir.

Q. Do you punch the clock there?

A. No Sir.

Q. What then?

A. I washed my hair before I left the plant due to the fact that I had been involved in particularly dirty work and left at approximately 4:55pm.

Q. Did anyone see you wash your hair or leave the plant?

A. I couldn't say. Probably two or three fellows from the shop would have been in there and would know about it.

Q. Did you go directly home from the plant?

A. Yes, sir.

Q. What time did you arrive home?

A. Not later than 5:20pm.

Q. Was there anyone at your house when you arrived there?

A. My family.

Q. Anyone else there?

A. No.

Q. Do you recall what you had for supper that evening?

A. No sir.

Q. Was supper ready when you got home?

A. I would say within 15 minutes – it usually is. We vary sometimes from night to night.

Q. Did you stay home that evening?

A. Yes Sir.

Q. Did you have any visitors at your house?

A. Not to my knowledge.

Q. Did your wife or any other member of your family leave that night?

A. No.

Q. In other words, you were home as a family group the entire evening?

A. That's right.

Q. According to your statement, you would have us believe that although you were in the Douglas Avenue area attempting to pick up some girls you were not connected with the Jeannie Singleton case?

A. That's right. My main reason for coming in and turning myself in is the simple fact that I have got to live with myself, and it is getting pretty hard to do.

Q. At the time you were attempting to pick up this girl, how were you dressed?

A. In the usual UpJohn clothing for maintenance3 men which consists of a light grey shirt, no tie,
and slightly darker grey trousers, all cotton.

Q. Where is your uniform now?

A. I have five or ten of them. Sometimes we change every day. If the suit you are wearing happens to be soiled, it was put in the laundry.

Q. In other words, the suit you were wearing that day has now been laundered?
A. That's right.
Q. Despite sometimes wearing your uniform for day, the suit you were wearing that day had been immediately laundered?
A. That's right.
Q. You were driving your car which you described as a 1953 dark blue Chev. Where is that car now?
A. At my home.
Q. Do we have your permission to search it?
A. Yes, certainly.
Q. What is the license plate of your car?
A. Chevy, license N.D. 16-32.

After reading the transcribed statement and signing it in front of Detectives Dykehouse and Gerlhof, Edgerton was booked and confined to the city jail. It was while he was in jail on this charge that officers asked if he would be willing to take a polygraph examination to prove his innocence in the Singleton Case. He agreed.

Edgerton wasn't prepared to come face to face with a person from the past, Officer Frank Thompson from his High School days. We were lucky enough to spend the day with now-retired Detective Thompson, to discuss this case. Frank described Edgerton's expression as that of "someone who saw a ghost" when the men looked at each other. Edgerton now realized that someone in the police department knew him. Conscious of the reasoning for why Edgerton was at the station, Thompson stated he showed no form of chumminess to this man. Edgerton stared hard at Thompson and then nervously looked away as he was led down the hall to his holding cell.

At 8:30am the following day, Edgerton was taken to the Michigan State Post in Paw Paw, Michigan by detectives and given a lie detector test administered by Detective Sgt. Victor Beck. Two graphs were being run at the time. In both cases according to Sgt. Beck, there were definite signs of deception.

Edgerton angrily denied any involvement with the Singleton girl and demanded a new polygraph to be administered.

He received his wish and was escorted to the East Lansing State Police Post that same afternoon for an additional polygraph with three graphs running simultaneously instead of two. When his results still showed deception Edgerton was interrogated once again. Because of the lateness of the day the suspect was lodged in the Ingham County Jail in Mason, Michigan for the night as he was still demanding yet another test.

The next morning, Edgerton was hooked up for his third polygraph test administered within a twenty-four hour period. This time it would be Lieutenant Peterman giving the test. Not surprisingly this test also resulted in the same results. Since he had confessed to the crime against Malinda, he was returned to Kalamazoo where he was charged with a city ordinance for molesting females. He was allowed to see his family, his attorney and his minister before being lodged back in jail.

With Edgerton back in jail, the men went about the task of substantiating his alibi. Not one person at UpJohn could validate seeing Edgerton between 3:00pm & 5:00pm, not even his supervisor. After returning to the station later, that night Detectives were given eight evidence bags and three glass vials containing articles which had been found in Edgerton's blue Chevy. The evidence was to be sent to Lansing; however, officers were already excited by the evidence. The technicians had vacuumed up pine needles and sand from the driver's side floor of his car. Obviously, Edgerton had been to a location recently that was full of pine trees.

Unfortunately, with no direct proof tying Edgerton to Jeannie's murder, he was released from custody.

His trial for accosting Malinda Miller was held on September 5th at which time he was promptly found guilty. He was sentenced to time served, $100 fine, $26.26 in court costs and two months of probation. Believe it or not, Edgerton started proceedings to appeal his sentence, but someone along the way made him realize this was not a smart move.

The Holland Evening Sentinel newspaper on October 21, 1955, ran a small update of how Edgerton dropped his appeal of the conviction. Newspapers also mentioned that he was cleared of any complicity in the Singleton crime. This statement might look good in the newspaper, but the truth of the matter was Edgerton was never cleared of anything; he remained their top suspect.

Almost a month after Edgerton came under suspicion for Jeannie's murder an Allegan, Michigan waitress came forward with some additional information about Edgerton. Juanita Thompson was employed at the Grays-dale Inn about one mile north of Allegan on M-40. On Monday, May 23, 1955, Juanita had a customer that she identified as Edgerton enter into the restaurant and order a cup of black coffee.

She claimed she kept an eye on him as he seemed to be nervous and slightly upset, but what stood out most in the waitress's mind was when this man stood up after drinking about 1/3 of his coffee and left the establishment without paying. Juanita mentioned the man who stiffed her for the 10 cent cup of coffee to her manager and continued with her work. It wasn't until Edgerton's photo ran in the newspaper for his arraignment that she realized who her stingy customer had been. She immediately called the police.

Detective Gerlhof took down Juanita's statement about her encounter with this man and validated her story by talking with the cook and manager who were on duty that day. They both joked that if a customer stiffed Juanita for an order, she would never forget their face. A check of her time card showed she had worked 10:00am to 6:30pm. When questioned about what this customer was wearing she stated he was wearing a tan or grey shirt and slacks. Juanita was certain she could pick this man out of any picture or in-person lineup in a minute! The Singleton case file never mentions if the police took her up on that offer or not.

There is now an eyewitness account of Edgerton being in Allegan County during the 5 o'clock hour on the day Jeannie disappeared. This was a tip Detective Gerlhof could not ignore, especially after they found Edgerton held a huge connection to Allegan County, particularly the Plainwell area.

Stanley Byron Edgerton was born on December 6, 1925, to Eugene and Locille Edgerton. The parents' marriage was turbulent one as Locille filed for and was granted a divorce, on the grounds of cruelty, just three years after the birth of their son. A 1930 Census shows Eugene Edgerton already married to another woman with 7-year-old Eugene Jr. in tow. Quite obviously the "cruelty" was partially due to another woman. Locille never remarried and carried the Edgerton name until her death on Christmas Day, 1986.

Locille and her son moved in with her widowed mother Ida Smith in Plainwell, Michigan. Locille's father, Seymore, had died of pneumonia in 1909. From the time he was 3 years old until his graduation from Plainwell High School, Edgerton roamed his hometown and the township of Gun Plains.

Retired Officer Frank Thompson attended Plainwell High School with Edgerton and remembered him as a "likable fellow" he went on to state further "that there was always something strange about him." During our interview, Frank showed us a 1943 Yearbook that showcased Edgerton as Class President, President of the Honor Society and participant in the Drama Club.

Upon graduation from High School Edgerton enlisted in the Air Force during WWII and was stationed at Fort Sheridan, Illinois. He was honorably discharged, returned home, and met his soon-to-be-wife Jeanne Ruth Hoffine. They were wed on October 22, 1949, and resided in Kalamazoo, Michigan.

Detectives became even more intrigued by the fact that Edgerton grew up in Gun Plains Township, the same township where Jeannie was taken to and murdered. The officers clearly remembered the small two-track road they had to find to get back to where the little girl's body had laid. They remembered discussions from that early June day about how only someone who was familiar with the area could have known this small gravel trail was here. The officers now had chills thinking about this; Edgerton knew this area. This was a coincidence that just could be ignored. Even today this road is hard to find and easy to miss. Rob's mother lives in the area on Pine Lake, and even though we have driven by the road hundreds of times; we never noticed it until we discovered this case.

Frank Thompson told us about a woman who came forward years later and stated she and a "friend" of hers saw Edgerton near Blakeslee Street on that fateful day but never came forward because her friend was a married physician whom she, despite being married herself, was having a torrid affair with. Frank said he considered it to be a valid sighting. We too have been contacted by people that know this nurse. There is no reason to doubt her sighting.

Edgerton was repeatedly interrogated in the coming year about his possible involvement in the Singleton case. In 1956 tiring of the questions he decided to move his family out of the area. He put in for a transfer with UpJohn and relocated to Arizona where he lived out his days.

The stigma of Jeannie Singleton couldn't be left behind, however. He still received many phone calls from the Kalamazoo area. These calls came from the police; he received several over-the-phone interrogations for years to come.

In 1973 Frank Thompson was shocked to receive a phone call from Edgerton, this call was made all the more stunning by the fact that Frank had an unlisted phone number and never could figure out how Edgerton had gotten a hold of it. Their conversation soon turned to the topic of Jeannie and Frank is positive to this day that he nearly had Edgerton ready to confess. When we asked him if he still felt Stanley was the killer he responded by saying "I don't think he is the killer, I know he is. I just wish I could have proved it."

In 2012 Michigan State Police Cold Team Detective Sergeant Michael Spring and his supervisor Detective 1st, Lieutenant Chuck Christiansen traveled to Arizona to speak to a "suspect" face to face. They were careful to not name the suspect. However given the fact that Stanley always has been the prime suspect coupled with the fact he was still living in Arizona at that time, there is little doubt who it is they went to question.

When interviewed by Rex Hall for a May 25, 2015, Kalamazoo Gazette article on the 60th anniversary of the abduction Detective Spring said the man in Arizona was a "very, very good candidate," and Detective Chuck Christiansen was quoted as saying he believes "they were looking face-to-face with Jeannie's killer."

Malinda Miller works with a sketch artist to develop a composite.
Photo courtesy of MLive Media Group, Kalamazoo Gazette, and WMU archives.

Composite drawings created of the attempted kidnapper.
Photo courtesy of MLive Media Group, Kalamazoo Gazette, and WMU archives.

Stanley Edgerton surrenders himself for questioning.
Photo courtesy of MLive Media Group, and the Kalamazoo Gazette.

A small portion of the statement given by Stanley Edgerton
Page taken from police case files.

Stanely Edgerton sits in jail during questioning.
Photo courtesy of MLive Media Group, Kalamazoo Gazette,
and WMU archives.

CLOSURE DENIED

The largest and most complex question remaining is why was this case never solved? There is not one simple answer. There are several answers that all lead to the unfortunate facts in this case. Jeannie was brutally murdered, and her family never learned the identity of their daughter's killer. Family and friends feel the pain of injustice over a crime someone was never punished for, and the Kalamazoo community lost their innocence and faced a new level of fear for their own children.

As stated many times in this book and probably best said by MSP Detective Michael Spring, "the 1950s investigators lacked the type of science and forensic tools detectives have at their disposal today. That the case involved an apparent stranger abduction was an anomaly too since most abduction and killings, 90 - 95% involve someone known to the victim."

Despite the massive amount of evidence that points to Stanley Edgerton, it's all circumstantial. Despite failing lie detector tests multiple times, polygraphs are not allowed to be entered as evidence. Edgerton was witnessed by multiple people cruising the neighborhood where Jeannie disappeared. He admitted to trying to pick up the 14-year-old girl for immoral reasons. He attempted to pick up a younger girl earlier that afternoon at Lincoln school for the same immoral reasons. Unfortunately, Jeannie was probably the last girl left walking home, and with Jeannie's gentle nature and habit of talking to strangers, Edgerton could have easily taken advantage of that unconditional trust and lured her into his car.

Edgerton's alibi for the time in question, 3:20pm-5:45pm on May 23, 1955, could never be substantiated. The work clothes he had on that day were immediately laundered that day despite the fact it is well known that he usually wore the same uniform for a couple of days before washing it. In his own words, he claimed he wouldn't wash his uniform unless they were "very soiled." Edgerton couldn't account for a single action that day at work that would cause his uniform to become that filthy; the girls he attempted to pick up that afternoon never made any reference to his clothes covered in filth or grease.

Edgerton entered into the Gray-dale Inn in Allegan County and apparently stiffed the waitress not only her tip but for the coffee as well. He would never give a reason why he was in Allegan County that day when he claimed he was at work and then traveling home.

Edgerton grew up in Gun Plains Township, the same area where Jeannie was murdered. He would have known all the little back roads and secret make-out spots in the township. Detectives said it themselves in the case file, only someone who knew the area completely could have known the dead-end two-track road existed.

A forensic search of his vehicle brought forth pine needles and sand; something Edgerton never could give an explanation for.

Since the day he walked into the Kalamazoo Police Department he became authorities' No. 1 suspect. Everything pointed to him, but nothing concrete was ever able to be produced to present to the prosecutor for charges. The one needed missing link never surfaced for an arrest.

One last tidbit we found in the Singleton case file that was extremely interesting is a lone mention of a name from a 1962 memo. That small line read in part: "Deputy Edgerton from Allegan County will check to see ……" Allegan County Sheriff's Department had a Deputy Edgerton in the early 1960s? I know the Deputy was not Stanley but could have this officer been a relative? That is yet another small mystery that may never be solved.

This brings us to the other possible suspect, George Fox. It's hard to throw away that possibility since he decided to brutally rape his wife in the same area as where Jeannie was murdered. Is it possible this man simply suffered from paraphilia? Paraphilia is a sexual disorder in which recurrent sexually arousing fantasies are necessary for sexual excitement. He could also be a compensatory rapist; a rapist who rapes in response to intense sexual arousal initiated by specific and often violent stimuli.

No one will ever know for sure why this attack took place in the same location. However, the location where Jeannie was discovered was public knowledge, and not much was done after the fact to secure the area. By the end of 1955 everyone knew where she was murdered. A man like George would find it hard to avoid visiting the area.

Obviously, George Fox was a sick and deranged individual who got off raping his wife and others. It is important to note however that aside from his wife's accusation there was never any evidence to tie Fox to the Gun Plains area or the Douglas neighborhood. He was also never on the extensive lists of suspects. If Fox knew his wife suspected he was capable of killing a young girl, that knowledge could become a powerful mental tool he could use to control his wife. Several people in the Kalamazoo area used the same threats including Fred Davis. Fred was never considered viable suspect by detectives either, however.

Now, you may be thinking of DNA testing. Why can't they test evidence collected from the crime scene? We asked that very question of Detective Spring. He informed us that although several items from the crime scene were saved, the evidence disappeared sometime throughout the years. His exact answer was, "Since it was a Kalamazoo City case originally I think the property would have gone to them but the body was found in Allegan County, so they were also involved. Since this was 1955, I am just not sure where the property was stored, but none of the departments involved seem to have any property from this case."

One thing we can't help but wonder is this. Could Deputy Edgerton from Allegan County have been a relative of Stanley and in some twisted sense of family "helped the evidence to disappear?"

This will remain one of those tragic cases where true justice will never be served. The world will never be able to say, "Here is Jeannie Singleton's killer!" We are forced instead to continue to use the politically correct terms alleged, believed or suspected killer due to legalities. How unfair to a small girl named Jeannie.

We can say this, however. It is the belief of several members of the law enforcement community and the authors that Stanley Edgerton is Jeannie's killer. As authors, we are not tied by the red tape used by the law enforcement community. We have the liberty to look at the evidence, draw a conclusion, and publish it without risk of it damaging our careers or the investigation. I hope everyone can rest a bit easier knowing that Stanley is now deceased and will never again attempt to abduct anyone.

Due to crime investigation techniques of 1955, the scene was never properly secured. Here we see many people trampling the crime scene.
Photo courtesy of MLive Media Group, and the Kalamazoo Gazette.

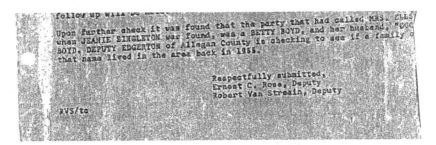

A portion of the memo mentioning Deputy Edgerton.
Page taken from the police case files.

SLOWLY LIFE WENT ON

Jeannie's abduction and murder opened the eyes of many in Kalamazoo. Parents who allowed their children to run wild through the neighborhoods suddenly kept their children closer to home. Jeannie's killer smashed any innocence the city once held. The illusion of "these things never happen in Kalamazoo" was shattered.

The school district immediately adopted a policy of contacting the parents when a child does not report to school, the "buddy system" was promoted, and parents lectured their children about "stranger danger." Many parents, sometimes with the help of local police officers, organized early versions of Neighborhood Watch programs. One such organization was founded by Kalamazoo native Duane Foote's mother. She called it "Mother's Block Watch." This organization watched the neighborhood children for many years following Jeannie's murder.

Dorothy and Steve Singleton moved their family out of Kalamazoo and into Van Buren County just a few years after Jeannie's murder. Their home at 1310 Blakeslee has been torn down for decades. The couple managed to stay together despite all the emotional strain; their faith never wavering.

Steve Singleton passed away on February 5, 1984, in Decatur, Michigan. He is buried near his beloved daughter Jeannie in Mt. Ever-Rest Cemetery on South Westnedge Avenue in Kalamazoo.

Dorothy Singleton continued to work for the Kalamazoo State Hospital for 22 years. She found happiness again after Steve's passing with Edwin Sheppard, whom she married. Unfortunately, Edwin passed a few short years later in 1989. She never married again, but she did, however, become a business owner in Van Buren County. She opened Singleton Adult Foster Care. Dorothy Singleton Sheppard died in October 2007.

Her obituary states she is buried in with her first husband and Jeannie, her grave marker remains unfinished; the date of death was never added.

Patsy Louise Singleton died of cancer on January 11, 1978, and was also laid to rest in Mt. Ever-Rest Cemetery. Her foster daughter Yvonne "Denise" MacDonald has become Jeannie's biggest online advocate, making sure a little girl's tragic legacy is not forgotten.

The rest of Jeannie's siblings grew up, got married and raised children of their own. Steve Singleton Jr. is currently suffering from Parkinson's disease and is suffering some memory loss; he still, however, has not forgotten his little sister, nor does it seem he ever will. When we interviewed him, it was clear he can still clearly remember his beautiful sister.

Life as it always does goes on. We may forget the smaller details like the way Jeannie laughed or the sound of her voice, but Jeannie lived on through the members of her family and dear friends. Watching from above, she followed her loved ones' victories, heartaches, special times, and holidays; she was never far away from the family that lost her so tragically.

Rest in peace, little angel.

APPENDIX –
FUNERAL HYMNS

"Beyond the Sunset"

Beyond the sunset,
O blissful morning,
When with our Saviour
Heav'n is begun.
Earth's toiling ended,
O glorious dawning;
Beyond the sunset
When day is done.

Beyond the sunset,
No clouds will gather,
No storms will threaten,
No fears annoy;
O day of gladness,
O day unending,
Beyond the sunset,
Eternal Joy.

Beyond the sunset,
A hand will guide me
To God, the Father,
Whom I adore;
His glorious presence,
His words of welcome,
Will be my portion
On that fair shore.

Beyond the sunset,
O glad reunion,
With our dear loved ones
Who've gone before;
In that fair homeland
We'll know no parting,
Beyond the sunset
For evermore!

"Follow Me"

I traveled on a lonely road, and no one seemed to care.
The burden on my weary back had bowed me to despair;
I oft complained to Jesus how folks were treating me,
And then I heard Him say so tenderly,
"My feet were also weary, upon the Calvary road;
The cross became so heavy, I fell beneath the load,
Be faithful weary pilgrim the morning I can see,
Just lift your cross and follow close to me."

"I work so hard for Jesus" I often boast and say
"I've sacrificed a lot of things to walk the narrow way,
I gave up fame and fortune, I'm worth a lot to Thee."
And then I hear Him gently say to me,
"I left the throne of glory and counted it but loss,
My hands were nailed in anger upon a cruel cross,
But now we'll make the journey with your hand safe in mine,
So lift your cross and follow close to me.

Oh Jesus if I die upon a foreign field someday,
'Twould be no more than love demands, no less could I repay,
"No greater love hath mortal man than for a friend to die"
These are the words He gently spoke to me,
"If just a cup of water I place within your hand
Then just a cup of water is all that I demand.
But if by death to living they can Thy glory see,
I'll take my cross and follow close to Thee.

ACKNOWLEDGMENTS

We would like to take this opportunity to thank people for all their help with this book. Heartfelt gratitude goes out to the members of the Singleton family and Jeannie's childhood friends for sharing your cherished memories. We would like to thank the Prolo family for your hospitality and for informally adopting us into your family. We can't forget to thank Robert Holderbaum for all of his help. A special thanks to retired Officer Frank Thompson, our afternoon spent with you was a real treat! We will never look at Kalamazoo the same way again.

Our gratitude is additionally extended to the following people who supplied help along the way – Michigan State Police Detective. Sgt. Michael Spring, Rex Hall Jr. from the Kalamazoo Gazette, Western Michigan University Archives, and members of the Vanished Kalamazoo Facebook Group.

ABOUT THE AUTHORS

Nicole and Robert Du Shane are the authors of the Paranormal Michigan Book Series. While conducting research for the sequel to their local bestselling book, Haunted History of Kalamazoo, they stumbled upon the 30-year anniversary article for a 1955 unsolved murder. The information uncovered was so enthralling it soon became the focal point for a new book about this almost forgotten murder. The authors hope this book will help breathe new life to a stalled investigation.

Nicole Du Shane is the founder of the West Michigan Ghost Hunters Society. She delved into the paranormal world at a young age. Growing up in a house where the former owner had committed suicide, Nicole began to research the phenomenon that was surrounding her on a daily basis. Eventually, her passion of the paranormal led her to start one of the best known investigative teams in Michigan. An avid fan of true crime stories and tragedies, Nicole created the Michigan Tragedies Facebook page.

Robert Du Shane is the founder of WPARanormal Incorporated. He grew up in a Portage home where seeing Indians roaming about was almost a nightly occurrence. Robert never suspected at the time that the spot where his house sat was once the site of a major Indian Massacre! Robert's interest in the paranormal flourished, and in 1993, he founded what would later become Michigan's first incorporated paranormal investigation team. This interest eventually led to the creation of WPARanormal Talk Radio in 2003.

Printed in the USA
CPSIA information can be obtained
at www.ICGtesting.com
LVHW042254021023
759939LV00004B/72

9 781626 769588